# Preparing For Financial Success

*Dedicated to my sister, Jane Park, whose willingness to proofread has made this book a better read*

Also by James Park

Dividend Investing: A Guide to Building Sustainable Passive Income

The Self Made Investor
www.theselfmadeinvestor.com


ISBN-13: 978-1-7339722-2-2
ISBN-10: 1-7339722-2-6

Disclaimer: As investors, we assume risk in order to obtain a return. This book is geared towards controlling for risk by investing in markets that have a history of providing strong long-term returns. However, we cannot guarantee the future of any market or the performance of any fund that is used to track a specific market. We invest at our own risk. We can take measures aimed at achieving the highest return possible for a given level of risk, but the risk of loss, nonetheless, will always be prevalent.

## About the Author

James Park is a CPA who has worked in the accounting profession for a number of years. He has a BS from Franklin University and an MBA with a focus on finance from The Ohio State University. Investing has always been one of his many passions. He believes in a self-directed, low-fee approach that relies on asset allocation and rebalancing. When the right asset classes are invested in for the long-term, the odds of the stock and real estate markets are undeniably stacked in the investor's favor. When sustainable dividends are added to the mix, the investor should feel comfortable that the income will persist indefinitely. His philosophy is that investing should be simple, and good information should be available to all investors.

**Table of Contents**

## Introduction

I'm glad you're here. It means you want to be successful with your finances. Or perhaps you're already successful and you want to learn more. That's even better. I'm a strong believer that no matter how skilled you are in a certain area, there's always room for improvement. There's always more to learn. That's why I read constantly. Not just about finance, but about business. The two go hand-in-hand. A successful business has to offer products and services that people need, and they have to do so in such a way that they maintain a competitive advantage.

There's more to running a business than developing and delivering a product or service. It has to be financially sound. And there are literally hundreds of ways to secure financial soundness, all depending on how the business is financed and the environment in which it operates. That's the part about business that not every entrepreneur wants to deal with. There are a lot of talented people with amazing ideas. But a business is a business, and those amazing ideas need to be combined with sound financial management. It's about more than how good the product or service is; if the business can't manage its finances, it won't succeed.

In many ways, each and every working adult functions like a business. When we enter the workforce, we strive to sell our time and skills for an attractive salary. Or maybe it's not money we're passionate about, so we sell our time and skills to an accommodating employer or to a worthy cause. We all have different reasons for getting out of bed in the morning. But for most, the bulk of the week is dedicated to some form of work that earns money. That's the first part of the equation. Just like a business provides a product or a service, working adults do the same. We sell our services to an employer, and in return, we collect a paycheck. From there, we're responsible for managing the money. And our success with this second part of the equation is completely decoupled from our success at work.

I can't help you with the first part, because this isn't a book about occupation; it's a book about achieving financial success with the money earned from your occupation. But in most fields, the better you perform at work, the higher your potential earnings. And that's important.

*Preparing For Financial Success* is about what you do after you've brought the paycheck home. It's about both your lifestyle and your ability to earn a return on your savings. Budgeting is the foundation for success. Earning a strong return on your investments is also important, but first you need to set money aside in order to make those investments. It's not a one-time sacrifice. It's a repeated process that forces you to increase both your invested capital and the stream of income you earn from that capita.

There are a lot of people who don't invest because they're afraid of the stock market. Maybe they started investing right before the 2008 financial crisis, and then decided that *"I'm not going to make that mistake again.*" Perhaps they watched their parents get scared and sell in the middle of a recession. Or maybe they think it requires unachievable mathematical and statistical skills to plot investments.

The truth is, investing is really easy. Even when you make mistakes—*which you will*—it's still incredibly easy for the long-term investor to achieve strong returns. If you understand this but still don't make investments out of fear, then the only thing holding you back is yourself.

Even more surprising is the notion that making good investments isn't the most important part of achieving financial success. The stock market's average rate of return when measured over extended periods of time comes in at roughly 10% (or 7% if we adjust for inflation). So if your goal is to make perfectly average investments, you can still expect to earn strong returns. What a lot of people don't understand is that it's better to be an above average saver and a perfectly average investor than it is to be a perfectly average saver and an above average investor. Over time, the more you invest, the greater the likelihood that your performance will to conform to the market average. But the more you save, the further ahead you'll be.

We're not shooting for the stars. Stories of stock market millionaires who turned $500 into a fortune are just that—*stories*. Our approach is different. And achievable. *Preparing For Financial Success* is about implementing sound money management techniques, and then relying on time-tested investment strategies to build long-term wealth. It's not a get rich quick scheme, but rather a playbook for responsible money management.

Some investments will perform better than others. And some will prove not to be good investments at all. This happens to every investor. It's easy to compensate for a few poor investments with a strong budgeting and savings regimen. But it's nearly impossible to compensate for a lack of savings with superior returns on the stock market. Most investments do not provide exponential returns. And the ones that do are both scarce and difficult to identify. In fact, if they were easy to identify, so many people would buy them that it would drive up the price to the point that the superior returns vanish. This is a phenomenon known as herd mentality. And we're going to learn that any time an opportunity for superior stock market returns can be exploited, the herd will behave in such a way that the benefit is lost. That's exactly what happens when an unknown company starts to shine. The herd gets on board, and they buy the stock up until the benefit of getting in "early" is lost. With thousands of unknown companies floating out there in the ether, it's pretty near impossible to identify the ones that will eventually start to shine. The strategies discussed in *Preparing For Financial Success* are not aimed at finding these needle-in-a-haystack investments, but are instead aimed at building wealth from predictable long-term market patterns.

We're going to walk through each and every step of the investing lifecycle, from budgeting and saving to restructuring our portfolio once we've built the kind of wealth that needs to be protected.

In *Chapter 1: Is $1 Million Enough?* we're going to start by setting a goal. The question each and every one of us needs to ask is, *how much money do I need to accumulate before I can retire?* For most of us, that's what retirement is; *it's a number, not a date*. Employment opportunities that provide a pension or some form of defined benefit plan have become scarce. In the profit-driven sector, these plans are nearly extinct. Most employees pay into a 401(k). They receive a tax benefit and a match from their employer and then they're on their own. They can't retire just because they reach a certain age. *But they can retire once they've accumulated* *enough resources!* A sense of safety is lost as defined benefit plans fall by the wayside, but having the ability to take control of your finances is very empowering. With effort, you can do better than what a defined benefit plan would provide. That's what *Preparing For Financial Success* is all about. We'll start with a goal. In *Chapter 2: Budgeting,* we'll lay the foundation for achieving that goal, and then we'll spend the next five chapters outlining our investment strategy.

If you read my first book, *Dividend Investing*, then you're already familiar with the strategy, and you've seen how dividend income can be used not only to increase the size of your holdings, but can also serve as a stream of sustainable income throughout your retirement. *Dividend Investing* makes a great companion to *Preparing For Financial Success.* But in this book, we're going to do more than just implement a winning investment strategy; we're going to examine the process of accumulating wealth from cradle to grave. We'll set a goal, we'll budget, we'll invest, and then we'll measure our performance. In *Chapter 8: Why it Works,* we'll dive deeper into our strategy and explore the theory behind the process. I don't want any readers to follow along blindly. I want you to gain a solid understanding of why the investment strategy advocated in both *Dividend Investing* and *Preparing For Financial Success* works. You'll learn about investment models that were designed by Eugene Fama, a Nobel Prize winning economist from the University of Chicago School of Business. You'll also become acquainted with modern portfolio theory (MPT), a framework designed by Nobel Prize winning economist Harry Markowitz. By the time you're done with chapter eight, you'll understand material that's taught to finance students in just about every MBA program across America.

In *Chapter 9: Benchmarking,* we're going to learn how to measure performance. It's easy to buy a stock and then compare its performance to the S&P 500. This is the most common benchmark in the investment world. But what you really want to know is, *am I on track for retirement?* Beating the S&P 500 won't necessarily get you to retirement, especially if you don't save enough. And if you do save enough, it's possible to stay on track for retirement even if your investments lag the S&P 500. We of course want our investments to perform well in relation to the appropriate index, but meeting our retirement goals is the primary objective. It comes down to a combination of both saving and investing. In chapter nine, we're going to revisit the goal that you'll be setting in chapter one, and we're going to develop a process for measuring your performance against that goal. This is the most important benchmark you can implement. In addition to measuring your investments against the market, you'll also be measuring the performance of yourself against your goal.

We'll set an additional benchmark while we're at it. Beating the market is great. In fact, keeping pace with the market is all it takes to build a solid retirement. But there will be times when the market doesn't provide positive returns. When this happens, measuring your dividends can provide a psychological benefit. When markets perform poorly, buying opportunities abound, and the dividend yield on those opportunities can be impressive. At the end of the day, what we really care about is the stream of income that our investments provide. The size of your portfolio might shrink during a bear market, but the dividend income may very well increase. The dividend conscious investor measures their dividends. They take pleasure in watching them increase from one quarter to the next, and they understand that bear markets present an opportunity to increase their stream of dividend income by leaps and bounds.

By the end of this book, you'll have a thorough understanding of the roadmap that takes you from earning an income to building a portfolio that delivers persistent and sustainable returns. You'll know how to build wealth. But education doesn't stop there. In order to be successful you need to keep learning. The investment world isn't static, but constantly evolving. I'm glad you've made the decision to read *Preparing For Financial Success.* But don't let your learning stop here. My success as an investor is attributable to the fact that I'm always reading and learning more. In addition to reading the books that I write, I encourage you to also read the books that I read. In *Chapter 10: Further Reading,* I provide overviews of the ten books that hold the greatest influence over my investment strategy. You can read them with the same strategy in mind, or you can use them to implement or refine a strategy that works best for you. There's no single path to wealth. But the path that I'm going to share with you already has footprints. Others have used it with great success. These are time-tested techniques that work. Just ask any retired investor who's implemented a strategy structured around budgeting, dollar cost averaging, asset allocation, and periodic rebalancing. This is the path that we're going to discuss. And I wish you the best in your journey.

# Chapter 1

## Is $1 Million Enough?

### Set your goal

We're going to start with a goal, and that goal should be a numerical goal that represents the amount of wealth you need to accumulate in order to be financially secure. We all want to accumulate enough money that continuing to work becomes optional. It will feel amazing once we get there. But we also want to feel secure as we progress towards that goal. Watching our portfolios grow is an invigorating experience. And when the markets work against us, knowing how to weather a storm is truly liberating. But first, we need to determine the number that makes us feel financially secure. And then we need to make progress towards that number. It sounds simple enough. But there are variables to consider, and with variables comes complexity.

It's possible that you're already building streams of income for retirement. You might not even be doing so by choice. They take social security out of your paycheck whether you like it or not. Many employees will contribute just enough to a 401(k) to meet their employer's match. And that's it.

*Yes, I know, I sound cynical.* But it's not because I think you have a poor savings regimen. It's because statistically speaking, this is what most Americans do. They pay their social security, they take advantage of their employer's match, and then they live life to the fullest. Or they're saddled with obligations that feel uncontrollable.

The fact that you're reading this book means that you want to do better. And you can do better. But it doesn't mean you need to stop enjoying life and focus completely on your finances. It means that you should only spend money on things that truly bring you value and enhance your life. In *Chapter 2: Budgeting,* we aren't just going to talk about ways to eliminate all of those unnecessary expenses; we'll also talk about structuring those expenses in a manner that increases the benefit while reducing the cost. Think of your life as a whole. And think about the enjoyment you want to extract from that life. Does it make financial sense to take a luxurious vacation now, when each dollar you spend would earn a return over the next 20 or 30 years? Or does it make more sense to do something less expensive now, and let your money earn a nice return before embarking on that expensive vacation? If you view life as a whole, you get the vacation either way. But the impact on your finances is different. If you're patient, and structure accordingly, then over the course of your life you get much more than a vacation. And that's what we're after.

This is the type of thought pattern we want to implement. There's a fine line between letting life pass you by and spending too much on unnecessary wants in an effort to live life to its fullest. Knowing where to draw the line is just one of the variables we'll discuss. But before we talk about spending money, let's analyze the retirement plans you've paid into and estimate the stream(s) of income you might already be expecting.

Most of us have social security and perhaps an employer-sponsored 401(k) plan. But your situation might be different. Maybe you're paying into a pension plan and also have a 457 plan. Or perhaps you've been funding an IRA account on your own. Whatever the case, it's important to incorporate the cash flow you expect to receive from each of your plans or accounts into your projection. This allows you to gauge the additional wealth that needs to be accumulated in order to secure the success that you're after.

When analyzing our streams of income, we need to consider inflation. For the retirement investor, this is one of the most important variables that we'll encounter. In fact, inflation is the reason why the chapter is titled *Is $1 Million Enough?* Because in all likelihood, it's not.

When you hear the word millionaire, you likely think of wealth. At least my generation does. That's because when I was a child, being a millionaire was associated with owning yachts and a private jet. The word still makes me think of Bruce Wayne and Tony Stark. But $1 million isn't what it used to be, and when it comes to retirement, $1 million might not be enough—*and that's assuming you're close to retirement age*. If you have 20 or 30 years to go, it's an even smaller amount.

It's difficult to predict what inflation will be between now and retirement. And it's equally difficult to predict what inflation will be throughout your retirement. The best we can do is review historic inflation trends and use them to make an estimate about the future. In all things investment related, past performance is never a guarantee of future performance. But when it comes to making predictions about the future, it's better to include an estimate for inflation than to not include an estimate for inflation. So let's go ahead and make an estimate.

We're going to consider inflation trends going all the way back to 1949. I've selected this range because it's 70 years long, so even the investor who just turned 20 should have confidence that this horizon is long enough to encompass the breadth of his investment career (from starting the portfolio up to the day when the remainder of the portfolio is bequeathed). This timeframe also includes the financial crises, which is good, because we know that we're going to face obstacles along the way. It's just that we don't know when, or how severe. The range does not include the Great Depression. And while there's no guarantee that we won't experience another economic downturn of this magnitude, it should be acknowledged that regulatory oversight has evolved.

During the financial crisis of 2008, the banks were bailed out. A $700 billion trust was established to relieve them of toxic assets. The Emergency Economic Stabilization Act of 2008 was controversial, and it's estimated to have cost $4,635 per working American. But stabilization was nonetheless implemented. I'm not going to take a stance on the ethical nature of the situation. As an investor, these things are beyond my control. The best I can do is digest what happened, and then make projections that consider the possibility of it happening again.

If we analyze data stretching all the way back to 1949, we see that the highest level of annual inflation is 13.3% and the lowest level of deflation is 2.10%. The average for the period is 3.4%, and we're going to use this average as an estimate moving forward.

Let's say you plan to retire in ten years. How much money will you need ten years from now to have the equivalent of $1 million today?

If we assume an inflation rate of 3.4%, you'll need to accumulate $1,397,029 in ten years to have the spending power that $1 million provides today. In 20 years, you'll need $1,951,690. And in 30 years, you'll need $2,726,567.

If you just turned 20 and plan to retire at 65, you'll need at least $4,502,194 in order to compare yourself to the millionaires of today. The best advice I can give is to start saving. It really is that important. But at the same time, don't feel overwhelmed by these numbers. Yes, they're gigantic. But don't underestimate what you can accomplish when you have time on your side. If you have 45 years to invest, the markets will bring you some nice returns, and you're going to learn that your investments will eventually do the work for you. It's a building game and it takes time, but it's also very achievable, so don't be scared by a big number floating out there in the distant future. We're going to break everything down into very digestible pieces. And then you'll strive to make progress towards that goal with each and every paycheck.

But first, you need to set your goal. You need a number. And it's not necessarily going to be $1,397,029 or $1,951,690 or $2,726,567 or even $4,502,194. These numbers were provided for the sake of illustration. Your number will be a factor of many variables, including your other sources of retirement income and the kind of lifestyle you want to enjoy.

## The typical investor

Even though the number is different for everyone, the investment world treats us as though we're all the same. In other words, the investment world likes to come up with rules. And too many of these rules are built around cookie cutter investors.

By "cookie cutter," I mean the typical investor. I'm sure you know her quite well. She lives in a quiet suburb with her husband and their 1.9 children. And they love animals. So much so that the family has 1.6 dogs, 2.1 cats, and 2.3 birds. Sometimes it feels expensive, especially when you consider that they have $16,425 in credit card debt. But they strive to pay this down, which is a manageable yet intrusive goal on their combined household income of $56,516. Thankfully, they live in an area where the cost of living is also incredibly average. Yes, everything about this woman and her household is incredibly average, and the financial world is flourishing with black-and-white advice for investors just like her.

We're all supposed to keep six months worth of salary on reserve in case of an emergency. When we build our budgets, they tell us to spend 50% on needs and 30% on wants, while the remaining 20% goes to savings. And when we invest that savings, we should treat our age as a percent and allocate that much of the portfolio to bonds. The remainder, of course, should be invested in stocks. Once we reach retirement, they tell us to follow the 4% rule, all because history shows that it will take 30 years to deplete a portfolio if you only spend 4% per year. It all feels very mechanical, which is understandable when you consider that that's how it's presented to us.

It's good to have rules. They keep us on track, give us a reference point when making decisions. But one 30 year period can vary significantly from the next. If, on average, we spend 30 years building our portfolio, followed by 30 years depleting our portfolio, we'll learn from experience that times change and financial markets change along with them.

The 4% rule is an important rule. I'll make reference to it throughout the book. But I'm also going to poke some holes in it, and the other rules too. *It's not that the rules are bad . . . they're just very cookie cutter.* A cash reserve keeps us safe. A proper budget helps ensure that we live within our means. The employer 401(k) match is essentially free money. Bonds insulate our portfolios against a stock market crash. And there should be a limit to how much we spend in retirement.

The only problem is that none of us are in the exact same situation. We have different incomes and different expenses, we have different time spans until retirement, and we have different wants in terms of lifestyle (both now and in our golden years). We'll discuss each of these differences throughout the book. But one thing that we all have in common is that we need a number. We need to know how much wealth to accumulate before we can retire. And we're going to use the 4% rule to help us get there.

**The 4% rule**

*So what exactly is this rule?*

Well, the 4% rule was popularized during the 1990s. The premise is that you should be able to withdraw 4% from your portfolio during your first year of retirement, and then adjust the amount for inflation as you make subsequent withdrawals. By sticking to this rule, your savings should last 30 years. The formula is based on historic market returns and assumes a 50/50 allocation between stocks and bonds. In other words, if you retire at age 65, you should be financially secure until you reach age 95.

The average American has a lifespan of 78.6 years. *So that's great!* The average American is covered by the 4% rule. However, there's a nearly 1/3 chance that at least one member of a 65-year old couple will live past age 95. And there are currently 55,000 Americans living today who have already surpassed the age of 100. People are living longer and life expectancy is increasing. Even if you fit a demographic that should be covered by the 4% rule—*that is, you have adequate savings and expect to pass before age 95*—there are additional variables to consider.

The rule doesn't account for other sources of income. Some Americans have pension income. Some have earned more social security than others. And some really need to stretch that 4% as far as it will go.

The rule also doesn't take your desired standard of living into account. But that's okay, because there's a cookie cutter rule for that too. Most financial advisors recommend that you build the resources to replace 70% of your pre-retirement income. If your household income is $60,000 going into retirement, then you should put yourself in a position where the 4% rule will allow you to spend $42,000 the first year of your retirement.

This kind of makes sense. The house is paid off, the kids (*hopefully*) are out on their own, and you're no longer saving for retirement. So in theory, your expenses should be relatively low.

*But what about medical bills?* That's another big variable. It's a gigantic unknown that makes all the difference in the world. Even the healthiest of people are eventually blindsided with an illness. If you're lucky enough not to incur large medical expenses before retirement, it's quite possible that your luck will change. It is currently recommended to have $200,000 set aside to cover out of pocket medical expenses throughout your retirement. So if we again account for inflation at 3.4% per year, in ten years you'll need $279,406, in 20 years you'll need $390,338, and in 30 years you'll need $545,313. If you just turned 20 and have 45 years to go, you'll need $900,439. And again, this is just for out of pocket medical expenses, not for a full retirement.

This isn't chump change. It's smart to start saving now. It's also smart to build medical costs into your retirement budget. Yes, the mortgage has been paid off. But medical bills can be immobilizing, and it might not be your only added expense.

For starters, you have a lot more free time in retirement. It's easy not to spend money throughout the day when you're working. But retirement is different. You want to enjoy life and you don't want to be confined to your home any sooner than you have to be, so you might find yourself spending more money on leisure activities.

On the plus side, you won't have to dedicate resources towards your retirement savings. That work should already be done. So if you were saving 20% of your take home pay, you don't need to do that anymore. *Or do you?*

It really depends on how much you enjoy saving and investing. The fact that you're reading this book indicates at least some interest. If you can go as far as to call it a passion, then read the next paragraph carefully.

They've done studies that show investors who were the most serious about building their portfolios have the most trouble spending them down in retirement. That's because they didn't just build the portfolio out of necessity, but because they truly enjoyed the process. It's only natural that they'll want to continue with the enjoyment through retirement.

In other words, investing is a hobby you might want to continue with throughout retirement. It's a hobby that requires money, but it's also a hobby that provides a sense of security. The ultimate goal is to reach the point where you can live off of your dividend income, *and then some . . .*

If you can satisfy the 4% rule with dividend income alone, then you'll never eat into the principal. And that's a great place to be. As we move into the chapters on investing, we'll see that consistently earning dividend income of 4% throughout retirement can be a challenge. There will be periods when it's achievable and there will be periods when it's not. So maybe you need to accumulate a nest egg that allows you to survive on dividend income of 3%. Or maybe you're comfortable eating into the principal. We'll discuss different scenarios, but it's up to you to decide what works best for both your personality and your situation.

The notion that you'll be able to live off of 70% of your ending salary might be a bit far fetched. It's contingent on your salary, so it's difficult to implement a cookie cutter rule that's applicable to everyone.

In all honesty, I don't think the average American should be satisfied with just 70% of their final salary come retirement. It's like you're getting rewarded with a pay decrease after all those years of hard work. But if you don't plan ahead, that's the reality.

Maybe it's better to aim for a portfolio where a dividend yields somewhere between 3% and 4% provides a stream of income equal to 80% of your ending salary. Or maybe more. It's different for everyone, not just in terms of how much you need in retirement, but in terms of the resources available to help get you there.

**Time for an example**

Let's go ahead and strive for retirement income equal to 80% of your ending salary. If your ending salary is $60,000, you'll need to multiply this amount by 0.8 and subtract your other sources of retirement income. Say you're entitled to

$25,000 per year in either Social Security or pension income. The calculation is as follows:

(60,000 x 0.8) – 25,000 = 23,000

This means that $23,000 needs to come from your portfolio during your first year of retirement. So if you plan to follow the 4% rule, your portfolio needs to be worth at least $575,000.

23,000 / 0.04 = 575,000

Just a tad over 52% of the income is coming from either social security or pension benefits.

25,000 / (60,000 x 0.8) = 52.08%

The good news is that Social Security beneficiaries receive annual cost of living adjustments, so if a large portion of your income will come from Social Security, you're covered. The bad news is that more and more pension programs are starting to implement an inflation cap, if they adjust for inflation at all. If you're receiving any type of payment that does not adjust for inflation, then you might need a larger portfolio so that the 4% per year also accounts for cost of living adjustments not earned on your other income.

When you get down to what the 4% rule is intended to accomplish, it allows the investor to deplete the account over the course of their retirement. If you build a large enough stream of dividend income, you won't have to spend much, if any, of the principal. And that means you'll be able to bequeath the bulk of your portfolio to a loved one. The best part is that you don't have to worry about outliving your assets. It's an ambitious goal that can be accomplished in one of two ways. You can either save a lot more during your working years, or you can structure your investments to provide above average dividend yields, maybe even as high as 4%. In *Chapter 6: Dividend Income and The Power of Compounding,* we'll discuss ways to get that extra boost to dividend yield. But for now, let's finish formulating the goal.

**Projecting your ending salary**

Anyone can just assume an ending salary of $60,000. But if you have 20 years until retirement, how do you go about formulating your estimate? My recommendation is to be conservative. Assume your pay will keep pace with inflation and nothing more. If we project inflation to be 3.4% per year, then go ahead and assume that your annual pay increases will also be 3.4% per year. If you get a promotion along the way, then it's icing on the cake, and you can adjust your plan as such events occur. Even if you're a highly motivated employee who's certain that a promotion sits in their future, it's better to adjust the plan along the way than to prematurely build the expectation of a promotion into your plan. It makes the process less stressful. The promotion you're after may come later than expected, or the company might undergo restructuring. If your projection includes increased earnings that never materialize, it's difficult to compensate for the shortfall.

We already know that we can compensate for average investment performance with above average savings, but it's extremely difficult to do the opposite. Remember, the more investments you hold, the greater the likelihood that your returns will conform to the market average. Being conservative pays off more than you realize. And from a psychological perspective, it's better to increase your forecast as you incur successes than to reduce your forecast based on a delay in your projection of those successes.

If you currently earn a $60,000 salary, the conservative approach is to include annual pay increases equal to our projected rate of inflation, which is 3.4%. This will leave you with an ending salary of $117,101 in 20 years. If your goal is to live off of 80% of your ending salary, you'll need your various streams of retirement income to provide an initial cash flow of $93,681.

Estimating your streams of income shouldn't be difficult. If you're working towards a pension, it's likely that you receive periodic statements that include an estimate of your benefits. The same applies to Social Security. You can create an account and monitor your projected Social Security benefits at https://www.ssa.gov/myaccount/.

We'll assume benefits are expected to be $65,000 per year. So a 4% yield on your investment portfolio needs to provide $28,681 in income during the first year.

93,681 – 65,000 = 28,681

In order to follow the 4% rule, you'll need a portfolio balance of $717,027.

28,681 / 0.04 = 727,027

And let's not forget about those out of pocket medical expenses. The current estimate is that you'll need an extra $200,000 in retirement. So if we again assume inflation at 3.4%, in 20 years, you'll need $390,338. So what you really want to strive for is a portfolio worth $1,107,365. That's the goal. In this situation, you're striving to build a portfolio worth $1,107,365 over the next 20 years.

So the answer to our question—*Is $1 million enough?*—is no, it's not enough. If you retire tomorrow, you might need less than $1 million. Depending on your other retirement benefits, you might need a lot less than $1 million. But if you're retiring in 20 years, chances are you'll need more. Perhaps you'll need a lot more. That's why you need to set a goal, so you know what you're working towards. And in this scenario, the goal is $1,107,365.

The good news is that you don't need to save the entire $1,107,365. We're only going to invest in asset classes that have a history of always beating inflation when invested in for prolonged periods of time. So rest assured that your money will be working for you. Historically, the stock market has provided average returns of 10% (or 7% when adjusted for inflation).

If we look at how the stock market has done over the past 20 years, we see that long-term returns can certainly add up.

In fact, this 20-year period is particularly significant because it encompasses both the dotcom bust and the financial crisis of 2008. Even with two significant market pullbacks, the market appreciated by 115%.

It's also important to note that this chart only tracks valuation. It doesn't account for dividend income. The investor who reinvested their dividends along the way would end the period with a gain of 212%. These dividends are reinvested at all points in the market cycle. So it's actually good for the market to spend some time in bear territory. It means that those dividends are reinvested at low prices.

What we're really concerned about is where the market might be when funds are withdrawn. In this example, the market has experienced a tremendous bull run, but also spent the better part of 2018 and 2019 trying to figure out which direction it wants to move next. And that's the thing about the stock market. It's easy to see where it's been, but difficult to predict where it will go next. Over the long-haul, we're confident that it will go up. But in the short-term, your guess is as good as mine.

It's quite possible that the market will be in bull territory when it's time for you to make a withdrawal. It's also possible that the market will be in full bear territory when you need your money back the most. That's why we want to only investment money that we don't need back in the short-term, which is typically defined as five years or less.

A bear market is defined as a pullback of greater than 20%. Although a bear market is never pleasant, the investor who has been in the game for 20 years when she needs liquidity likely won't lose any money. Instead, her investments will have appreciated so much that she's simply giving back a portion of her gains.

If the investor builds enough dividend income that she doesn't have to sell any shares, then the act of having to sell into a bear market can be avoided entirely. But getting there is easier said than done. The possibility that you will some day be forced to sell into a bear market is very real. We'll spend plenty of time discussing a strategy aimed at negating this outcome. But for now, don't be intimidated by the goal that you've set. Yes, it's probably a big number. But the stock market can provide some hefty long-term returns. *All you have to do is invest in an ETF that provides broad market exposure, and those returns will be easily achieved!*

## Determining your projected rate of return

*So how much do you need to save each month in order to retire with a portfolio worth $1,107,365?* It depends on the expected rate of return.

It's easy to look at historic stock market returns and assume a 10% rate of return moving forward. But remember, this is an average, meaning that about half the time, actual results are below the average. So if all Americans were to calculate the amount they need to save each month based on average historic stock market returns, we can expect that half of them will not be prepared for retirement.

So again, we're going to cast a conservative projection. And if you beat that projection, then you'll end up with even more than you need (or perhaps retire younger than you anticipated). It might even be enough to take a cruise around the world, buy a vacation home, or leave your loved ones a larger bequeathment, all depending on your preferences. At the same time, if returns are less than the historic average (which is a very possible outcome), you'll at least have enough for a comfortable retirement.

Let's start with 10%, the historic average rate of return. And let's assume that deviations from the average can be plotted along a normal distribution.

These graphs might remind you of the first statistics class you ever took. What this tells us is that 68% of the time, we can expect stock market returns to deviate from their historic average by as much as plus or minus one standard deviation.

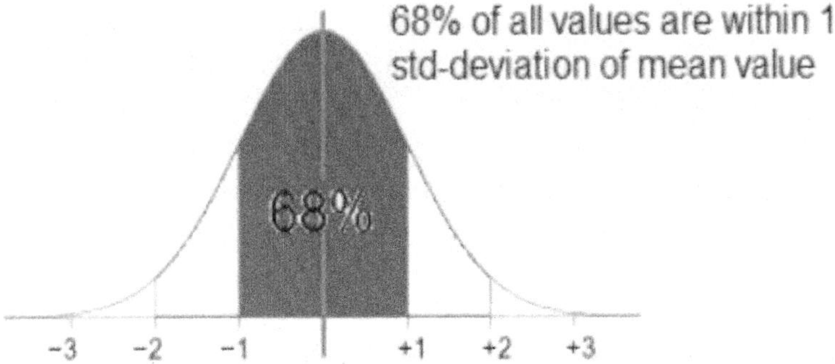


And 95% of the time, we can expect stock market returns to deviate from their historic average by as much as plus or minus two standard deviations.

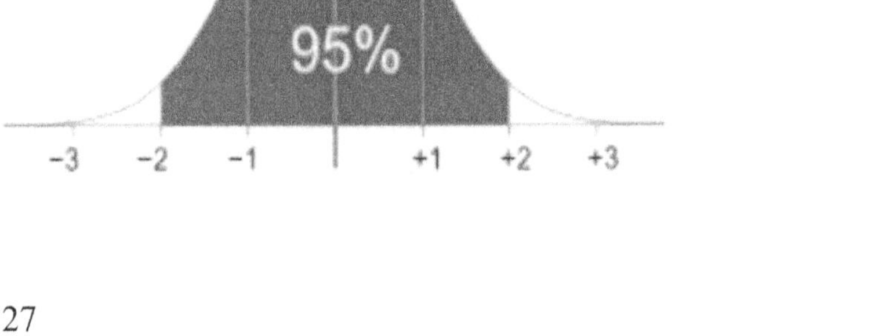

Finally, 99.7% of the time, we can expect stock market returns to deviate from their historic average by as much as plus or minus three standard deviations.

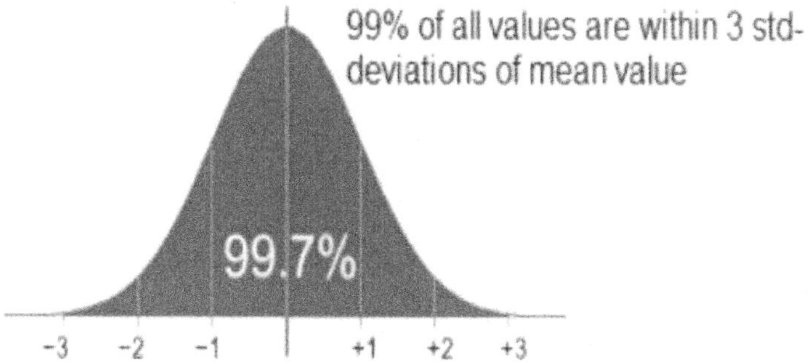


*So what does this tell us about the expected return on our investments?* We can't just assume a 10% rate of return because half the time, actual results are expected to be less than this. The optimists among us can argue that half the time, actual results are expected to be greater than 10%. But this is your retirement. Instead of gambling on the likelihood of achieving above average returns, we need to be prepared for below average returns.

The normal distribution warns that 1.5% of the time, stock returns will be three standard deviations below their average, 2.5% of the time they will be two standard deviations below their average, and 16% of the time they will be one standard deviation below their average.

For this to be meaningful, we need to know how large a standard deviation is. And it's different for every portfolio, all depending on the amount of risk that you're willing to assume. In *Chapter 5: Asset Allocation,* we're going to combine different asset classes in an effort to maximize returns while controlling for risk. This will reduce the size of each standard deviation, and consequently, insulate the portfolio against market setbacks.

If you choose to be completely risk averse and invest 100% in bonds and other fixed income investments, a standard deviation will be close to zero. You've locked in your returns, making it unlikely that you'll deviate from them. But the returns will also be small when compared to what you could have earned on the stock market, and it's unlikely that you'll earn enough for a comfortable retirement.

On the other side of the coin, you could take on high levels of risk in an effort to achieve even higher returns. By doing so, you increase both your upside potential and your downside potential. And this will be reflected with a higher standard deviation. A portfolio allocated 100% to emerging markets, for example, would have a higher standard deviation than a portfolio allocated 100% to the S&P 500.

Another way to evaluate standard deviation is by looking at volatility. The figures aren't static, but we can assume that a portfolio with low volatility might have a standard deviation around 3%, a portfolio with moderate volatility might have a standard deviation around 8%, and a portfolio with high volatility might have a standard deviation as high as 24%.

We'll assume moderate risk and therefore moderate volatility. You're trying to earn a return on your investments, but you don't want to take a bath in the process. In *Chapter 5: Asset Allocation,* we'll see that the amount of risk you want to assume decreases with time, and therefore, so will the volatility of your portfolio. For now, if we go middle of the road and assume moderate volatility, it means that there's a 16% chance that the average rate of return on your portfolio will be 8% below the average, for a total return of only 2% (10% – 8%). In other words, there's a small chance that your average rate of return will be very unsatisfying, and an even smaller chance that it will be negative. Three standard deviations at 8% comes to 24%. So there's a very small chance that your average rate of return will be -14% (10% - 24% = -14%). If you have a short investment horizon and end on a crash, an outcome such as this is very possible. But it's important to remember that the longer the investment horizon, the greater the chances that your average rate of return will conform to the historic average of 10%.

If you do invest for the long-haul and still come in, say, 0.5 standard deviations below the average, your rate of return will be 6%. An outcome such as this is very realistic. A conservative approach to plotting your retirement would be to assume a below average return of only 6%, knowing that it's possible, though unlikely, that average returns will fall below this level.

Over time, you'll adjust the holdings in your portfolio, and this causes the likelihood of achieving certain returns to change. In your early years, you should focus on investments that provide strong capital gains and moderate dividend income. As you approach retirement, with the goal of building a secure portfolio that yields 3% to 4% in dividend income, you'll switch to more conservative investments that provide smaller returns but stronger dividend yields. If your expected rate of return is again 6% and your dividend yield is 4%, then your investments will need to appreciate by an average of 2% each year in order to stay on target. This is a safe and achievable assumption, so long as you see things through during periods when returns are negative.

If you get scared and sell during a crash, you'll never make it to the finish line. It's like starting the race all over, except everyone else now has a head start. And given that you sold during the crash, the market will likely by higher when you get back in, so it becomes an uphill race in more ways than one.

It pays to be conservative and it pays to see things through. In practice, I use a projected average rate of return of 6.125%. I'm not going to gamble my retirement on hopes that market returns will keep pace with its historic average. But I also control for risk and will remain invested for the long-haul. I'm not concerned that my average rate of return will drop a full standard deviation (or more) below the historic average, but the possibility, albeit a small one, still exists. That's why in *Chapter 9: Benchmarking,* we'll focus on ways to measure the performance of your portfolio against your goal. And we'll discuss strategies to help get things back on track in case you fall behind at any point in the race.

**Determining how much to save each month**

*We've made progress!* We know that your goal (*in our example*) is to build a portfolio worth $1,107,365 over the next 20 years, and we know that actual stock market returns might fall below their historic averages. So I'm advising that 6.125% be used as the projected rate of return. Assuming a portfolio of moderate volatility, this puts us approximately, but not quite, 0.5 standard deviations to the left of the average. It's a conservative yet reasonable projection. And before we analyze the results, I'm going to make one more assumption. If we're looking at 20 years until retirement, then in this scenario, it's conceivable that you've already been working for 10 to 20 years. So let's assume you already have some savings and your portfolio will start with a balance of $200,000.

The question remains, how much do you have to invest each month in order to build a portfolio valued at $1,107,365, assuming an average rate of return of 6.125%? We'll need to take your goal of $1,107,365 and discount it backwards.

If you took Finance 101 in college, then you probably know a formula that will get you there. Or you could build an amortization table to help with your analysis. I'm a big fan of amortization tables, so I'm going to make things easy for you. If you visit my website—https://www.theselfmadeinvestor.com/store/—you'll be able to download a preformatted amortization table free of charge. In fact, I've made a number of tools available in one download. It's titled *Preparing For Financial Success Spreadsheets*. We'll rely on other tools in subsequent chapters. For now, we'll be working with the tab titled *Retirement Benchmark Tracker*.

In cell AE13, the table shows that in the first year, you'll need to contribute $695 per month to the portfolio, and then you'll need to increase this amount by 3.4% each year. In other words, we continue with the assumption that your salary keeps pace with our projected rate of inflation and that you correspondingly increase your contribution by the same amount.

In reality, your situation could be vastly different than what's illustrated here. If you have longer to go before retirement, then not only will you make more monthly contributions, but those contributions will have more time to grow. Your goal could be very different, and so could the amount of savings that you start with. For many, $695 in savings per month is ambitious. It's the equivalent of owning an additional car. This is why I can't overemphasize the importance of starting early. If it's too late to start early, start now. The longer you have until retirement, the less you'll need to save each month.

Maybe you'll aim for retirement income equal to the recommended 70% of your ending salary rather than striving for 80%. Or if you're really dedicated, maybe you'll shoot for 90%. That's why we have the amortization table. All of the yellow boxes in the Input table can be overwritten with different assumptions. I encourage you to play around with it. Enter different scenarios and see what the results look like. This is your opportunity to not only plan for your necessities, but to set expectations for what's possible. If you want an extravagant retirement, this is your chance to determine how extravagant, and also the amount of savings you need to sacrifice today in order to get there.

| Input | |
|---|---|
| First month investing | 1/31/2019 |
| Last month investing | 12/31/2038 |
| Beginning contribution | 200,000 |
| Monthly Contribution | 695 |
| Projected Annual Increase | 3.25% |
| Expected average ROR | 6.13% |
| Inflation/contribution increase | 3.40% |
| Project dividend / bond yield at retirement | 4.00% |
| Projected tax rate at retirement | 25.00% |

| Output | |
|---|---|
| Projected ending balance | 1,107,414 |
| Earnings to date | 213,889 |
| Required earnings | 212,222 |
| Over / (under) | 1,667 |
| Dividend income at retirement | 44,297 |
| Monthly | 3,691 |
| After tax dividend income | 33,222 |
| Monthly | 2,769 |

Column Y allows you to track your progress. At the end of each month, simply enter the value of your portfolio, and you'll know whether or not you're on track.

**Retirement Benchmark Tracker**

| Date | Beginning Blance | Monthly Contribution | Expected ROR | Return | Ending Balance | Actual Results | Over/ (Under) |
|---|---|---|---|---|---|---|---|
| 1/31/2019 | 200,000 | 695 | 6.125% | 1,024 | 201,719 | **201,756** | 37 |
| 2/28/2019 | 201,719 | 695 | 6.125% | 1,033 | 203,448 | **203,260** | (188) |
| 3/31/2019 | 203,448 | 695 | 6.125% | 1,042 | 205,185 | **205,513** | 328 |
| 4/30/2019 | 205,185 | 695 | 6.125% | 1,051 | 206,930 | **206,900** | (30) |
| 5/31/2019 | 206,930 | 695 | 6.125% | 1,060 | 208,685 | **208,785** | 100 |
| 6/30/2019 | 208,685 | 695 | 6.125% | 1,069 | 210,449 | **210,856** | 407 |
| 7/31/2019 | 210,449 | 695 | 6.125% | 1,078 | 212,222 | **213,889** | 1,667 |

If you feel like you can't possibly come up with the monthly contributions required to meet your goal, don't throw in the towel. In the following chapter, we'll focus on budgeting. The idea is to free up some extra cash in order to increase the size of our investments. But we want to do so in a manner that still accounts for our needs and the enjoyment we want to extract from life. It can be a challenge, but it will be a rewarding challenge if done right.

# Chapter 2

## Budgeting

Budgeting is the most crucial component to financial health. It doesn't matter if you're an avid investor or not. Your financial stability is at risk if you don't learn to budget.

I'll admit that budgeting isn't the most exciting topic. There's no action. It's not as dull as reading a dissertation on the history of taxation in colonial America, but it doesn't offer the kind of excitement we get from investing. When we invest, we turn money into more money. *And that's exciting!* When we budget, we take money we already have and make sure we don't spend it all. *See what I mean, not early as exciting*. But at least the government doesn't charge us a tax for implementing a sound budgeting strategy—and *shhhhhh*, don't give them any ideas, because I wouldn't put it past them.

A successful budget lets you know where you stand. It helps you decide if that luxury expense you want to incur is really in your best interest right now or something you'd be better off looking forward to in the future. In the end, a successful budget helps you save more, which allows you to invest more, and then you get to turn money into more money. So there will be some excitement in store, even though it's a delayed gratification.

You need to spend less than you make. That's the most important mantra to instill in your mind. So I'll say it again. *You need to spend less than you make!* The material contained in this book won't be useful if you can't do that, and your financial success will be stifled.

This is the easiest lesson we'll cover, and it's one that you don't really need a book to teach you. But we all benefit from the occasional reminder. As I said in the introduction, budgeting is the foundation for financial success. Without it, we won't have the funds to plant our investments, and we won't be able to watch the portfolio grow.

This is an area where you simply need to do better than others. That's how a secure retirement is created. The longer you invest, the greater the chance that your returns will succumb to the average. But the more you save, the greater the chance that your portfolio will be larger than average. I can't stress enough how important it is to start saving and make continuous contributions to your portfolio. You'll be rewarded for the effort.

This is also an area where some have it easier than others. If you have a large family or other obligations that currently force you to spend your entire budget, you might feel overwhelmed by the concept of saving. I'm going to encourage you to change your way of thinking. A budget that's exhausted every month is the kind of obstacle we want to be working with. It means that there are more areas where changes can be made and savings can be generated. Even a small amount of savings will become significant over time, so long as the strategy is repeated every month. And the more budget categories you have, the more you'll save if you can find an opportunity to cut back on each of them.

The kind of changes you make will be specific to what you want from life. My job is to provide some food for thought. Your job is to figure out what works best for you.

**Is it all because of Starbucks?**

The internet is awash with articles on how to save money, and they're not very judicious in their process. They like to select common targets for their attacks, with your daily latté from Starbucks being first on the list. Yes, it's delicious. But at $2.95 a pour, even the gourmet roast from that fancy aisle in the grocery store looks like a bargain. You could save a fortune by brewing your own. Or at least $42,604.

That's right, if a Starbucks drinker bypasses their daily $2.95 latté, invests the money in equities, and achieves a conservative average rate of return of 6.125% per year, they will have an extra $42,604 at the end of 20 years.

If your goal is to build a portfolio worth more than $1 million, an extra $42,604 helps, but it's not going to get you there. So you'll have to come up with more expenses to cut back on. And maybe the little expenses aren't where you need to focus. Maybe all those articles on the internet should have picked a different target. I'm not going to criticize the successful money manager who builds a retirement portfolio by skimping on small purchases. These things add up. But are small expenses really the best place to focus your efforts? In the coming pages, we'll review some of the bigger expenses you might incur, such as your house, your car, and your vacations. Small expenses can add up quickly, but big expenses stand out on their own. So the real question is, can you find a way to get what you need without going quite so big on these expenses? A higher price tag means there's more to save if you can find a more conservative means of making the purchase.

Between your house, car, and vacations, what if you could save an extra $300 per month? If invested the same as the $2.95 we might have spent at Starbucks, at the end of 20 years you'll have an extra $142,443. If you do both, then you're almost $195,000 of the way to a successful retirement.

The types of expenses you hone in on in an effort to reduce your budget will vary according to your wants. You need to determine what's important and what's not. I'm not going to advocate in favor of (or against) the different expenses you may or may not reduce in an effort to save more. These are personal decision. But when it comes to reducing costs in an effort to squeeze more savings out of the budget, the big items hold the greatest weight. Your house, your car, the number and the type of vacations you take, these are all decisions that have a profound impact on your savings. And you'll cross the finish line sooner if you don't buy more than you need.

From a purely financial perspective, we all need to live within our means, and if your goal is to accumulate wealth, then you need to make efforts to live below your means. Whether you choose to live slightly below your means or substantially below your means is up to you.

### The 50 / 30 / 20 rule

Let's return to our typical investor. You remember her. She lives in a quiet suburb with her husband, their 1.9 children, and their 1.6 dogs, 2.1 cats, and 2.3 birds. The family is straddled with $16,425 in credit card debt, but they have a combined household income of $56,516. They're not just striving to pay off their debt, but to build some investments along the way.

The rules of personal finance were made for this woman. And I've already alluded to the 50 / 30 / 20 rule. She should allocate 50% of her budget to needs, 30% to wants, and 20% to savings.

The rule was developed by Elizabeth Warren, the senior United States Senator from Massachusetts, and her daughter, Amelia Warren Tyagi. They detail the strategy in their book *All Your Worth: The Ultimate Lifetime Money Plan*. It's an encouraging read that anyone interested in accumulating wealth will enjoy.

What I really like about the plan is that it's simple to implement and follow . . . *so long as you don't have big, fixed expenses that exceed 50% of your budget*. In other words, are the costs of your home and car within reach? Have you been blindsided with large medical bills? Are you still paying down credit card debt that you foolishly racked up in your 20s? Some situations are beyond control. And sometimes the financial decisions we make as young adults follow us for longer than we wish they would.

If your budget fits into this rule, *great!* You're on your way to a sustainable retirement. If not, do yourself a favor and cut back on the wants and not the savings.

The needs are mostly fixed costs. You have to have them. That's what makes them a need. If you can find a way to satisfy the need at a lower cost, then you're starting to think like a successful financial planner. If not, cut back on your wants and let your savings flourish. You'll be better off in the long run.

You might be thinking that you don't need to save 20% because you've already come up with a number and you know how much to save each month in order to get there. In chapter one you set a goal. You plugged your assumptions into the *Retirement Benchmark Tracker*. In our scenario, you need to save $695 each month, but maybe 20% of your take home pay comes in at $815. My advice is to go ahead and save the $815.

Think of the number we developed in the first chapter as a minimum. Based on our expectation of the variables we analyzed, we developed a minimum contribution that you need to make each month. If it's feasible to save more, than by all means do so. You never know when an unexpected variable will pop up, like a disability or other tragic event. Or the actual rate of return on your investments could come in lower than expected (*perhaps by an entire standard deviation, ouch!*).

The great thing about the 50 / 30 / 20 rule is, once you have the 50% that you spend on needs under control, the wants function as a variable cost. If you decide to spend less than 30% on wants during a certain month, you can. If the market is performing poorly—*that is, if stocks are priced at a discount*—you might decide to cut back on those wants for a few months and bulk up your investments. When we cover asset allocation, compounded dividends, and rebalancing, we'll see that there's never a bad time to increase the contribution to your portfolio. But if markets are down and you can skimp a little bit on your wants, the long-term return will be powerful.

If squeezing 20% of earnings out of your budget for investments is difficult, then you need to take a closer look at your budget. At a high level, there's two ways to go about this. You can spend less or earn more. A side hustle might be in your best interest. But as I state in the introduction, this isn't a book on occupation. If you take the side hustle route, there are plenty of books at your disposal that will aid you in transforming the skills you already have into an added source of income. But for purposes of *Preparing For Financial Success*, we're going to focus on the budgeting side of the equation.

Let's have a look at some ways to spend less.

**How much house should you buy?**

This is a good question. And it likely comes down to more than trying to save an extra $300 each month while you enjoy your daily latté.

For most, the mortgage is going to be the largest expense, but it's also an investment that will pay you back in the future. If you pay rent instead, it's still a large payment. And while you won't be getting a return on that payment, the amount of savings you accrue on repairs, taxes, interest, and insurance can be phenomenal. You can argue that you're paying these things anyway, because the landlord rolls all of his expenses into your rent, but the average renter is still paying less per month than the average homeowner. And the savings should not be ignored. If you don't want to rent forever, delaying the transition to homeownership can create a profound advantage. It might even save you that $300 per month from the example above. Just make sure that you're responsible with the savings and that you don't put yourself in a position where you eventually enter into a 30-year mortgage and find that you're still paying it off in your 70s.

Some of us are already locked into a mortgage, so we're forced to structure our budget around this large recurring payment. If you have yet to buy a home, do yourself a favor and don't buy the most expensive home that the realtor says you can afford. This is the easiest place to reduce expenses, so long as you only buy as much home as you need.

In fact, I applaud the decision to buy *all* the home you need, and nothing more. *And it's not because you don't really need a big home if you'll be spending a large quantity of time feeling very awake and energized at Starbucks.* It's because the more expensive the home, the more expensive the cost of maintenance. It's never wise to sacrifice physical comfort for money, though it's equally unwise to sacrifice financial comfort for luxury. And the tug of aware between physical and financial comfort is profound when it comes to buying a home.

Keep the home manageable and affordable. And from an investment standpoint, it's always better to buy the smallest house in a nice neighborhood than to buy the largest house in a not so nice neighborhood.

The speed at which you pay down your home is another consideration. It generally comes down to interest rates. If you've locked in a low one, then you're better off paying the minimum, and whatever funds you would have allocated towards an extra payment can then be invested. But when mortgage rates get up around 6%, it's a judgment call. There's nothing worse than watching your portfolio tank while the bulk of your mortgage payment goes towards interest and not the actual home. And there's something to be said for owning your home outright. It provides both a sense of accomplishment and financial freedom. Paying in advance will initially reduce the funds you have available for investments, but having the home entirely in your name will provide a safeguard in the event of an emergency. Regardless of the approach, your home is likely to be the largest expense you'll ever incur. It pays to keep it reasonable. You'll be glad you did.

**Car payment**

Your car payment probably takes the second biggest bite out of your budget. In fact, we discuss this thoroughly in *Dividend Investing*. While owning your home outright will take longer, owning your car is much easier. It's a tug of war with interest payments. The strategy I advocate in *Dividend Investing* is that once you've paid off your car, keep driving it and start making car payments to *yourself* instead of the bank. If you're already used to making a monthly payment, then continuing to do so after the car is paid for shouldn't be a struggle. But here's the kicker—when you make that payment to yourself, you not only avoid paying interest, you get to be the one who earns the interest.

We've already seen what an extra $2.95 a day turns into over 20 years when you stop drinking Starbucks and start making investments. It's an extra $42,604. The same concept applies to every tiny ounce of savings that you can squeeze from your budget. When it comes to interest, if you can find a way to earn it rather than pay it, the impact is further multiplied. It can take a number of years to get to this point, but it will have a profound impact on your financial health.

**Smaller expenses**

Finding ways to save on big expenses makes a huge impact. The results are immediately apparent. But those smaller expenses can also add a punch. It's okay to extract enjoyment from small purchases. Drink the Starbucks if it makes you happy, but don't spend a dime on something that's not important to you. It only delays your retirement, especially if you have wasteful habits. Some of these small expenses come out of the 50% allocated to needs, others are wants, and some are difficult to categorize.

Historically, utilities have been a need. But these days the lines are blurry. When we start lumping cell phones, internet access, streaming services, and prime memberships into the basket, it's really hard to tell what's what. Not only that, but all of these costs add up quickly. Yes, it's expensive. But if you're already incurring all of these costs and looking for ways to cut down, it at least gives you something to work with.

You're always going to need gas and electricity, but there are ways to minimize these costs. Turn the lights off when you're not in the room. Listen to your gas company when they make recommendations on how to reduce your usage.

If you're subscribing to media, ask yourself if you're really getting your money's worth. *Is it really improving your life? And is there a cheaper alternative?* The library is a good place to start. It's a wonderful resource that's often underutilized. The next time you feel like going to the movies, try spending a day at the library instead. It will save you money that day, and perhaps considerably more in the future.

In addition to your necessities, what other small expenses do you incur? And do you really need them? Make a list and keep track of them for a month or two, then ask yourself if these items truly improve your life. How much are you able to squeeze out of your budget without feeling the pain? Once you've determined this, *go for it!*

**Hold a reserve**

It's easy to budget month by month and then throw everything you didn't spend at the stock market. In fact, doing so sounds like a wonderful idea. But your expenses don't always align with your earnings. Some months you might have a big emergency, other months you won't.

It's important to build a reserve into your budget. You might need to set $100 aside each month for the inevitable home repairs. Perhaps you're saving for a vacation, or maybe you can foresee that your children will need braces. Some of these expenses are wants, and others are needs.

Regardless of how you categorize them, don't let your reserves eat into the 20% that you're supposed to be saving. Yes, you're setting these funds aside each month, but it's not true savings. You're setting the reserves aside so they can be spent in the future. And given that this isn't true savings, it shouldn't be invested the same way that you invest your savings. If you have a short-term investment horizon, make sure the money is invested risk-free. You'll get a fixed rate of interest. Nothing too impressive, but the reserves will be there when you need them.

The car payment we discussed previously is an excellent example. Or maybe you'll eventually need to replace a piece of exercise equipment like a treadmill. And when all is said and done, those braces might cost more than you were expecting. It pays to set aside a fixed amount each month so that extraneous expenses can be incurred without infringing on your regular monthly spending.

This is also a good area to implement a strategy, because how much you set aside won't necessarily equal what you spend. The goal is to build an adequate reserve that provides a cushion for emergencies. You want to always have adequate resources available. But if you get to the point where throwing more money into the pot is no longer necessary, then it's time to redirect your monthly contribution towards your true savings. In other words, *it's time to invest!*

I advocate two different approaches for managing a reserve. You can pick the one that works best for you or you can implement a hybrid.

Say, for example, $200 of your monthly budget goes into reserve. The funds can be handled as follows:

1) Set a ceiling. The size of your reserve should be contingent on the size of your house, how often you vacation, and other periodic expenses you plan to incur outside of your monthly spending. You'll also want some extra padding for emergencies, and this might correspond to the size of your family. So take some time to fully analyze the types of extraordinary expenses you can expect, and then set a ceiling. The goal is to build your reserves up to the ceiling, and then for however many months you maintain the ceiling, the $200 will go to your portfolio instead. You'll still be contributing 20% of your take home pay, but now you'll be contributing more.

When you eventually spend out of your reserve, it will bring the balance down below the ceiling. You'll then need to stop investing the $200 each month until the reserve is replenished.

2) When the S&P 500 is above its 15-year moving average, put the full $200 into reserve each month. When the S&P 500 is below its 15-year moving average, put the $200 into your portfolio instead. We'll discuss dollar cost averaging in the next chapter, but if you're already familiar with the concept, then you'll understand the benefit right away. You should already be allocating 20% of your income to your investments. But there's an obvious benefit to allocating more. Whatever extra you contribute, there's an even bigger benefit to making the contribution when markets are trading below their moving average. The premise behind dollar cost averaging is that your money will buy more shares when

markets are down. If you are going to up the allocation (by throwing some of your reserves at it), you'll acquire more shares if you consistently do so when the market is below, rather than above, it's average. And you're returns over the long-haul will be impressive.

**What if I'm supporting a family?**

The needs and expenses of the typical family will always outweigh the needs and expenses of an individual. There's really no way around it. Finding ways to save while still making those contributions towards your child's 529 plan can be difficult. *Where does the 20% that I need to save for retirement come from? And then maintain a reserve? And try to squeeze extra savings out of the reserve too?* It's a lot.

Yes, you have more expenses. But that translates into more opportunities to cut back and make changes. Adopting a glass-is-half-full mentality can make all the difference. If you're feeding a family of five instead of a couple, it means that every way you find to save on groceries goes 2.5 times as far (5 / 2 = 2.5). If the family eats out four times a month and you decide to cut back to three times a month, you'll free up more cash than a couple who makes the same effort.

The question is, can you cut corners that don't make a huge difference, and then multiply the savings times the number of people in the family? Your budget might be full to begin with, so think of each item already in the budget as an opportunity.

You want to do a good job of providing for your family, but would it make a huge difference if your children each received one gift fewer at Christmas? It will make a difference to your retirement. And while Christmas can be an exciting time, material thrills are often short-lived, where the benefit to your portfolio will continue to compound and grow for the rest of your life.

It's easy to put saving for retirement off until the kids are out of the house, but that doesn't change the fact that a dollar saved today is worth more than a dollar saved tomorrow. The sooner you invest your dollars, the more time they have to grow.

At the same time, you can't simply stop being a parent. There are certain expenses that you and your family will only benefit from now. And once those years are gone, they're gone forever. It's your job as a parent to juggle and prioritize. My goal is to provide a thought process that allows you to hone in on what's truly important, and hopefully assist you in not spending money on things that aren't important. Your children are important. Paying interest rather than earning interest on your car payment is also important. But getting to the point where you can do that requires discipline.

If being a parent forces you to delay saving for retirement, then play around with the *Retirement Benchmark Tracker*. The formulas assume a steady increase to your savings that aligns with your projected rate of inflation. But if you're going to save less now and more later, you can override the formulas and detail a plan that's specific to your situation. Here's a hint. Whenever you override formulas, be sure that you're working with a copy of the spreadsheet and not the original. That way you can always return to the original spreadsheet (with formulas intact) should your plan change.

Does saving less now and more after the kids are grown get you where you need to be? If not, then you'll need to make some concessions. Only you can determine which concessions are in your best interest. So I'm going to encourage you to extract as much from this book as you can, implement a strategy that makes a difference in your current role as a parent, and then teach what you've learned to your children.

Think about it. This book is about building a stream of dividend income that will last through your retirement. What if your children were to start on that today? It might eat into however much time they spend playing video games, but if you can get them to dedicate at least some of their energy to long-term goals, the rewards will be astounding.

Let's say your child gets an afterschool job as soon as he starts high school. He'll have four years of savings under his belt by the time he gets to college. And if he stays at home, commutes to school, and continues working part-time until he earns his degree, he'll have eight years under his belt by the time he enters the real world. He'll have a nice little stream of dividend income to supplement his entry level salary, and he'll be able to use those dividends to take a nice-sized bite out of his student loans. He'll be way ahead of his peers, and the experience he'll have gained from working that afterschool job might be just as valuable as his education.

Like anything else, it's a sacrifice. Maybe instead of working an afterschool job, he wants to play hockey and glide around the ice in all that expensive gear you'll have to buy him. And maybe you as a parent think that the experience of being on a sports team will provide some of the life lessons he needs in order to develop into an educated adult.

This book isn't going to make that decision for you and your family; clearly, both options have their merits. What this book is going to do is encourage you to think about what you want out of life, plan for it, and understand the tradeoffs that you'll need to make as you work towards achieving your goals. But just because you're supporting a family doesn't mean that saving for retirement needs to sit on the back burner. No matter how small, finding ways to save is important.

**What if I'm in debt?**

For many, debt starts when we're really young and it can take years (*or even decades*) to erase. It funds our college, pays for our home, and can be used to buy a nicer car than the one we should be driving. And then it sticks around for a really long time and gets in the way of other endeavors.

There are two pieces of advice that I'd like to give on the subject of debt, with hopes that you'll take them into consideration as you strive to increase your stream of passive income.

The first is to never take on debt in order to obtain something that doesn't pay you back for having incurred the debt. A college degree, for example, will pay you back with (hopefully) a higher salary. A house will pay you back with free rent and (hopefully) capital appreciation. But that big screen TV that you're tempted to place on your credit card will never pay you back for the interest payments, and therefore, should never be purchased on credit. If you have to take out a loan to buy a TV, it doesn't just mean you can't afford the TV, but also means that you can't afford to pay interest on the TV. If your resources are scarce, all the more reason to make better use of them. It's better to earn even a modest amount of interest in a savings account than to incur unneeded debt.

The second piece of advice is to make informed decisions regarding how quickly you pay off the debt. Acquiring debt doesn't have to stop you from making investments, and depending on the projected return from your investments, paying the debt off quickly won't necessarily be in your best interest.

Whether it's student loans, your mortgage, or maybe a car payment, the debt you're carrying most likely has a set interest rate and a minimum monthly payment. Adjustable rate mortgages are an exception, and those should be refinanced if the interest rate rises higher than what you're comfortable with. You should always make the required payment per the terms of your loan. Once this is done, the decision to pay the debt down faster, thus reducing the interest paid over the life of the loan, should be directly related to your next best use of the money. Or simply put, if you weren't paying off the debt, what would you invest the money in? And is the return on that investment expected to be greater than the interest paid on the debt?

As we move into asset allocation and structuring our portfolios, we'll form a reasonable approximation for the amount of dividend income we expect to earn from our investments. If the expected rate of return on an investment exceeds the interest rate paid on your debt, then it's better to pay just the minimum due each month, and then go ahead and invest the remaining cash. But if your investment opportunities aren't very promising, or if you've taken on debt at too high of an interest rate—*perhaps as a result of maintaining a poor credit score*—then you're better off paying down the debt as quickly as possible, and funding your portfolio should wait until the debt has been eliminated.

There's no one-size-fits-all for debt. But I encourage you to allocate at least some savings to your portfolio each month. It's good diversification to invest in more than just owning a home. But it's also comforting to own an investment that's truly brick and mortar. When a recession hits, people lose their jobs and the stock market takes a turn for the worse. You can't live in your portfolio, but owning your home outright provides a sense of security that prevails through both up and down markets.

**Vacations**

Luxury expenses are extremely malleable. You don't have to incur them if you don't want to. So if there's room for them in the budget, you can think of them as a cushion. Indulge in them when you want, and then cut back on them for emergencies or to accrue extra savings.

Vacations are a perfect example. This is an area where you not only have the potential to really save, but to be forward thinking. This is what our non-working lives are all about. Some of us want to travel to foreign countries, others are content to enjoy local attractions. To the extent that your wants align to your budget, the world is your oyster. Define what makes you happy, and then structure that happiness so that it's not a financial burden.

What we're really talking about in this section is a thought process. We'll discuss the process in terms of vacations, but it's a process that can be applied to any number of luxury expenses.

*Where do you want to go? What do you want to enjoy? And how important is it to do so now instead of waiting?* If you can put immediate gratification aside and structure not just your vacations, but all of your luxury purchases around your financial framework, you come out ahead. You might have to be patient and travel abroad only when it makes sense, but over the course of your life, you'll have more if you structure your expenses strategically.

You might be tempted to take a trip to the Bahamas this year, but you get more out of life if you wait, earn a return on the cost of the trip, and then indulge. This is true of any experience that doesn't have a shelf life. And shelf life is an important consideration. The experiences we want out of life don't just come with financial considerations; there will always be logistical matters to contemplate.

Let's say relaxing by a pool in the Bahamas isn't your cup of tea. You'd rather backpack through Europe or spend a weekend at an incredibly expensive (or perhaps geographically distant) ski resort. These experiences are also expensive, and may be more feasible later in life. But the experience is also more meaningful in your youth. Some day you'll simply be too old to enjoy them. It happens to all of us. And no amount of wealth can buy back an experience that needs to be enjoyed in your youth.

Financially speaking, you lose all those years of returns if you don't put these wants on the back burner, take a cheaper vacation now, and invest the difference. That's the dilemma. And there's no way around it. Building wealth to enjoy physically intensive excursions later in life could prove to be a wasted endeavor.

That's what we really need to focus on when we budget. It's not just a monthly budget. We're building reserves. We're projecting pay increases that keep pace with inflation. And we'll come out further ahead if we think in terms of a lifetime budget. It's about more than the nickels and dimes. It's about prioritizing in a way that not only makes fiscal sense, but allows you to enjoy what want out of life before it's simply too late.

You can sit by a pool in the Bahamas once you're older, and you'd be foolish to sacrifice financial security just to do so in your youth. But backpacking and skiing? If these things are really important to you, then you need to make a concession. And if your finances are as important to you as they should be, then you need to make offsetting concessions on other wants that can be enjoyed later in life. Maybe you'll buy a lower end model car than you can otherwise afford, knowing that later in life, you'll be trading in your ski trips for a Tesla. It will give you something to look forward to while you're weaving around moguls at the Chamonix resort in France.

Once you're older, maybe you'll settle for a less expensive form of vacationing. A long weekend spent hiking at the nearest state park can be rewarding. And if you find yourself losing the wherewithal to enjoy such outings as you age, then you won't feel as though you allowed life to pass you by as you saved money for an experience that never materialized.

As much as I'd love to structure my activities in the order that makes the most financial sense, the simple truth is that there will always be things in life that need to be enjoyed now. Building wealth is a journey. But make sure you have some fun along the way.

When it comes to the wants section of your budget, make a list. Rank each of your wants in order of importance. And then re-rank them in order of expiration. This should help you determine what to focus on now, and what to look forward to in the future.

Strive to implement at least some of the strategies covered in *Preparing For Financial Success*, and then form the habit of thinking in similar terms every time you make a financial decision. The thought process of structuring your vacations in a way that makes both financial and logistical sense can be applied to other sections of the budget. Perhaps a vacation isn't even in the picture, but you spend countless evenings at the movies. *Are you watching new releases the Friday they come out or are you waiting six to eight weeks and catching the same flick at a discount theater?* If you love going to the movies, then there's no reason to stop, and waiting an extra six to eight weeks until it hits the discount theater is an extremely small concession to make for added wealth. It's not like putting your dream vacation off for another ten years.

And we've already seen that we can accrue an extra $42,604 by making small concessions.

Maybe you only save $10 at the movies, but you also save $15 at the grocery store, and then $25 by enjoying a bottle of wine on your back porch rather than at the local bistro. And then next month, you do it all over again. Think about all of the small concessions you can make. Just like your large expenses, rank them and prioritize them. You might be really surprised to see how the savings compounds with very little effort.

Success is the result of small actions repeated every day for an extended period of time. Little actions that don't cost you anything but save you something repeated over and over again will add up. When you throw in the savings on that vacation to the Bahamas you postponed, it's a huge leap forward. It all comes down to building a lifestyle that provides for all of your needs while making an effort to not spend money on things that aren't important.

**The 90-day foodie challenge**

I'm going to discuss another luxury expense. It might also be on your list of wants, or maybe it's not. Either way, I hope you find the material of benefit. As long as you walk away with a thought process that can be applied to other expenses, then we're moving in the right direction.

We're going to discuss food. But more specifically, we're going to discuss food as an experience. Being a foodie is expensive. Dining out can add up fast, especially if everything on the menu is amazing. It starts with a bottle of

Malbec. Perhaps an appetizer. Your dinner. A piece of tiramisu. Maybe even a cappuccino or a glass of Moscato to cap things off. And then there's the sticker shock when the bill arrives. We've all been there in one form or another. But when it comes to your savings, the real question is, *how often do you end up there?*

Hopefully I haven't made you hungry or eager to go to a nice restaurant. But just like the family that has more areas to work with when it comes to finding expenses to cut back on, so does the foodie. It's okay to enjoy these types of experiences. Build them into your budget if they make you happy. But keep an eye on how much of the budget is spent eating out, and make sure that it's contained within the 30% that you've allocated to wants. Although eating is certainly a need, dining out is a luxury, and it needs to be treated as one. And if you're trying to squeeze more savings out of your budget, this is the type of luxury you should start with.

Let me tell you what I did. I call it the 90-day foodie challenge. It's a great way to give an extra boost to your savings without making permanent lifestyle changes. Instead, you'll make those changes for 90 days, and then allow the benefits to compound for the rest of your life.

My wife and I tried this with great success. Although we love eating out, we decided to stop for 90 days. But we didn't stop enjoying ourselves. That's the important part. It's not about sacrificing enjoyment in order to save for retirement, it's about replacing enjoyment that strains your budget with a different enjoyment that doesn't strain your budget. Even if the effort is only temporary, the results are permanent. That's because the extra savings you accrue today will keep growing. Your investments will continue to pay dividends and your funds will continue to increase in value (so long as you hold them for the long-haul).

We did our 90-day challenge in the summer. We'd only been in our home for a couple of years, and our back patio had been underutilized. So we decided it was time to spend a summer at home. We loved the atmosphere, and it made us wonder why we hadn't spent more time out there to begin with.

We cooked more. We started bringing home takeout from healthy but inexpensive cafes. On the weekends, we enjoyed a reasonably priced bottle of wine from the grocery store. And not only did we discover new dishes, but we discovered new places to grab a quick yet affordable meal on the run. The best part, of course, is that we saved a lot of money. Even if we never do the 90-day challenge again, we managed to place more savings aside than we normally do.
It's important to factor savings into your budget, but it's also a good idea to ramp it up every once in a while. Do it in short bursts. Cut back on something you enjoy, even if it's only temporary, and then let the benefits compound. I like to think of it as building long-term investments with short-term sacrifices. And when I get tired of making the sacrifices, I stop. So long as we spend within our budgets, we don't have to make any sacrifices that we don't want to.

Everyone has to decide what's important to them, because life is about more than saving money. Sometimes you have to enjoy what you have. And for us, this is it. We'll sacrifice our vacations, even delay the purchase of a new car for as long as we can, because we're selective. We only want to spend money on things that improve our lives. And for us, eating out and trying new restaurants meets the criteria of a necessary want. But that doesn't mean we have to eat out every week, and we never let ourselves overpay for the experience.

The markup at restaurants is unbelievable . . . *but also well deserved.* They don't just provide a meal; *they provide an atmosphere.* They provide a server who tends to your needs. And in a sense, they provide a show. If you ever acquire a circus and can't find someone to run it, hire a restaurant manager. They're more qualified than you realize. It's a tough business. I know, because I worked my way through college as a line cook. Those were some of the best days of my life, and it's part of why I have such an affinity for eating out. I understand why restaurants charge what they charge. Like any business, they have to invest in inventory. But their inventory has a shelf life, and they can't run out of any ingredients if they want their customers to keep coming back. So there's a markup. And it's not just a markup on the cost of your plate, but on the cost of the entire show that they orchestrate each and every night.

As an adult who now sits on the other side of the table, I continue to understand the markup. And having worked in the industry, I tip well. But I'm also looking for ways to keep my expenses under control. The glass of wine on my back porch tastes just as good as it would at a restaurant (*especially when the weather is nice!*). And even when I go into a specialty store like Whole Foods, or shop in that aisle at Kroger where everything's higher quality but a tad more expensive, I'm paying significantly less than I would at a restaurant. Yet the food is still high quality. The difference is that the grocery store doesn't have to put on the same kind of show.

I'm glad my wife and I spent that summer on our back porch, not just because we saved money, but because we continue to incorporate it in our lives. As a consumer, I get to decide when I want to enjoy the full-service experience and when I want to enjoy a meal on my back porch. When I choose the former, it saves me a bit of money.

**Setting the right mindset**

There are literally hundreds of strategies that can be used to cut costs from your budget. And while strategies are good, having the right mindset is even better. We don't want life to pass us by as we save for the sake of saving, but we also don't want to spend unwisely and not be prepared for a future that will arrive faster than we expect.

The mindset I implement is to always remind myself that every time I misspend a dollar, I've just stolen from my retirement. And I've actually stolen more than just a dollar; *I've also stolen the appreciation that I would have earned on that dollar.* This doesn't mean I can't enjoy life, it just means that I only want to incur expenses that improve my life. If I go to a movie that I'm not really excited about just to see how it is, chances are good that it will make me feel like I wasted money. And that's exactly what I've done. In fact, that's how most impulse purchases feel. I've just wasted money, received very little, if any, enjoyment, and I would have been better off tossing the money into my portfolio. And if I practice this mindset, then I don't need to feel bad about spending money on the things I truly enjoy.

This isn't a hard concept to grasp. People who are focused on their financial wellbeing already know that they shouldn't waste money. But taking it a step further helps ensure that the right actions are implemented. If you spend money unwisely, you're stealing from your retirement. That's the truth of the matter.

The goal is to implement a mindset that doesn't make you feel uncomfortably frugal, and to evaluate each expense for what it is. Eating out twice a week can significantly delay your retirement. Enjoying a home-cooked meal on your back patio can help keep things on track.

**Budget by Category**

So far we've talked about ways to save in different categories and we've considered the impact of debt on the budget. Now we need to structure the budget. And this, too, is different for everyone. Some people like to keep a tight budget and then strive to beat it. Others like a more comfortable budget that allows some wiggle room. So long as the budget accounts for ample savings, either approach is fine.

Personally, I'm fond of over-budgeting. It's the approach that works best for me. I like to budget for the recommended 20% in savings, but then structure my finances so that I've over-budgeted, if only slightly, for each of my needs and wants. In some categories, it's as simple as rounding up. If I expect my cell phone bill to come in at $61.73, I go ahead and budget $65. In other categories, I budget for a worst-case scenario. If I expect to spend $100 every week on groceries, I might go ahead and budget $130. I find the approach to be psychologically beneficial. Even though I'm spending money on groceries, when I come in under budget, I feel like I've just made progress towards my retirement. It's a small amount, but over a lifetime it adds up.

Assuming my expenses aren't much higher than expected, I'll end the month with a bit extra. I generally put the extra savings towards retirement. This helps me beat the benchmark that we'll discuss in *Chapter 9: Benchmarking*.

This approach won't work for everyone. Some people feel inclined to spend their budget, and the result is that over-budgeting becomes synonymous with over-spending. If that's the case, you need a tighter budget. And if you want to save more, you'll need to budget the extra savings up-front.

## Budget-to-Retirement Calculator

I have another tool to help you achieve success. It's aimed at determining what you'll be able to save given your monthly budget, and it calculates what this savings will grow to over time if properly invested. The *Budget-to-Retirement Calculator* is included with the free download at https://www.theselfmadeinvestor.com/store/. Just like before, you can change the assumptions in the yellow cells to get a feel for how they impact your results.

| Input: | |
|---|---|
| Years until retirement | 20 |
| Expected average annual stock market return | 6.125% |
| Savings already accumulated | 200,000 |
| **Budget** | |
| Monthly Income | 4,150 |
| Mortgage | 1,200 |
| Car payment | 300 |
| Groceries | 400 |
| Utilities | 405 |
| Insurance | 200 |
| Entertainment | 400 |
| Reserves | 200 |
| Other | 200 |
| Savings | 845 |
| % saved (s/b > 20%) | 20.36% |

You'll see the impact of saving just a little extra each month. In cell AI18, you can enter the amount of extra monthly savings that you're striving for. Maybe it's an extra $5, an extra $25, or even an extra $100. Play around by entering different goals in this field and see what kind of impact they have on the end result. You'll be surprised at what just a little extra savings can grow to over a prolonged period of time.

**Budget-to-Retirement Calculator**

| | |
|---|---|
| Monthly Savings | 845 |
| Annual Savings | 10,140 |
| % saved | 20.36% |
| Expected final portfolio balance at retirement | 1,057,939 |
| Expected final balance if $1 extra saved each month | 1,058,414 |
| Total benefit of $1 extra | 475 |
| Specify extra amount to save each month | 25 |
| Expected final balance with extra amount | 1,069,809 |
| Total benefit with extra amount | 11,870 |

## A final word on budgeting

By the time you're done with *Preparing For Financial Success,* you'll be able to view your budget, your chosen lifestyle, and your long-term investing strategy in terms of a future reward. That reward is a portfolio that either pays enough interest and dividend income to support your retirement, or gets depleted slowly over the course of your retirement, based on the 4% rule. But you can't do the former without the latter. Without budgeting, there's no savings. And without savings there's no investing.

In the first chapter, we concluded that $1 million probably won't be enough, even though this amount has historically been associated with wealth. I'll share a secret with you. It's extremely difficult to save your way to being a millionaire. You can be as frugal as you want, but it's extremely difficult to become a millionaire on savings alone. That's why we invest. It's a combination of saving and investing that gets us where we need to be.

I hope I've provided the right foundation for budgeting and saving. Now let's take a look at investing.

# Chapter 3

## A High Level Overview of Our Strategy

If you read my first book, *Dividend Investing*, then you're already familiar with my investment strategy. It's a time-tested approach that eliminates the need to make judgment calls. Instead of chasing after short-term market movements, we're going to let the markets do whatever they darn well please. We'll learn to be perfectly content with whatever they happen to be doing at any point in time. And by sticking to our guns as the markets move through their cycles, we allow the markets to bring the gains to us. It's not as exciting as chasing after a hot new stock. But it's safer, it's consistent, and for the long-term investor, there's very little downside to worry about.

Most new investors think that the stock market is a trading game, that it's about getting in and out of the right stocks at the right time. *It's not!* In fact, with my approach, we won't even be picking stocks. We'll be relying on index funds.

There's only one Warren Buffett and there's only one Peter Lynch. If anyone else tries to sell you a book about how they turned $500 into $5 million over an incredibly short period of time, ask yourself why this person spends his time writing books. If he had a magic stock market formula, he'd be sitting on a beach in the Bahamas sipping on a cocktail. And chances are, so would you.

I don't have any special insight on what the market might do next. And a good financial advisor will tell you the same. Sure, it's fun to make predictions. But market movements are both random and reactionary. It's news releases that drives investor behavior. We can speculate on how many interest rate hikes we might receive before the end of the year, form hypotheses on how earnings season might turn out, or just make wild guesses. But at the end of the day, we never really know what the market is going to do next, just like we never really know what the next news release is going to be. Once the market makes its move, it's too late to place our bets. And that's really all there is to it. We can speculate that the market has momentum and will keep going up, or we can speculate that the market has moved as high as it can for the foreseeable future. *Or, we can implement an investment strategy that doesn't require us to predict market movements, and allow the gains to come to us.*

My formula isn't glamorous. But it's realistic. And if you use it the way I describe, the odds of succeeding are stacked in your favor. In fact, it's more of a strategy than a formula, and there's no magic involved. It's simply a collection of tools that can be used to build wealth over time, so long as you give the endeavor the effort it deserves. If you stick to the plan, the risks are incredibly small, while the rewards are large and will continue to compound for however long you allow them to. But it takes patience . . . *and effort.*

The best thing about this approach is that it's already stood the test of time. Academics have been developing these models since the 1950s. The results are good, they've been measured, and they're still applicable in today's market.

It's unfortunate, but an investment approach that has stood the test of time and continues to provide good results is actually quite rare. It all comes down to investor behavior, otherwise known as herd mentality. Investors are always studying the behavior of other investors. Some try to learn from them. Others try to outsmart them. The contrarian investor will try to predict herd mentality and then invest in such a way that it allows them to profit. And more often than not, they strive to profit by betting against the herd. Sometimes it works, other times it doesn't. The market isn't static, and when it comes to predicting short-term movements, what worked yesterday might not work tomorrow. That's why we're going to implement a long-term strategy. When investments are held for extended periods of time, herd mentality will only have a small impact on the results. Long-term returns are rooted in the health of the economy and we should expect them to be positive.

The funny thing about investor behavior is that you can't rely on it from one year to the next. As soon as a pattern emerges, investors will react in such a way that the pattern dissolves. Take the January effect, for example. This theory suggests that stocks will increase in price during January. The reason behind this is that everyone sells their losing stocks in December in an effort to claim a tax refund. They then re-enter the market in January, after having waited 30 days in order to buy back the same stock (the tax loss is forfeited if they buy the security back in less than 30 days, known as a wash sale). On top of tax harvesting and subsequent re-buying, it's also believed that more buying takes place in January as a result of investors receiving bonuses at work and subsequently placing them on the stock market.

So if market timers expect the herd to sell in December (causing prices to drop) and then re-buy in January (causing prices to rise), *how will they behave?* Most are going to do just the opposite. If prices are expected to drop in December, that's when they'll buy. And if prices are expected to rise in January, that's when they'll sell. It seems simple enough, but there's a big problem here. The more noticeable the January effect becomes, the greater the number of investors that will try to profit from having recognized the pattern. And this behavior will eventually have an offsetting effect. The act of selling against the herd has an impact on the market. When a growing number of investors begin to implement a contrarian approach, the impact increases. In other words, the herd is likely to change direction once a pattern is observed. Now everyone is buying in December and selling in January. And this means that everyone who just tried to profit off of the January effect ended up losing money.

A pattern is only profitable until it's noticed, and there are plenty of examples of this phenomenon. Take, for example, the filter system. Stock traders are often advised to purchase a stock after it has increased in value by 5%, because a 5% increase indicates momentum. Similarly, they are advised to sell if it eventually decreases in value by 5%, because a 5% pullback indicates the beginning of a downward trajectory. This approach is called a filter system, and the percent used doesn't have to be 5% (that's just an example). The point is that this kind of system causes patterns to form, and the herd will take note of the pattern. It will work at first, but as more follow suit and the herd gets bigger, the benefit will dissolve. Eventually, buying will cease after a stock rises 5% (preventing it from moving higher) and selling will cease after a stock declines by 5% (stopping it from falling further). Those who are still trying to buy and sell when this happens will find themselves losing money.

The January effect and the filter system are based on market indicators that make sense, and they work until the herd follows suit and behaves in such a way as to eliminate the benefit. But not all market indicators make sense. Sometimes "investors" come up with theories that are just ridiculous. Take the Super Bowl indicator, for example. This indicator suggests that if an NFC team wins the Super Bowl, a bull market will follow. If an AFC team wins, we're stuck with a bear market. Surprisingly, the indicator has been right more than it's been wrong. In fact, it was almost always right until the 1970s when Leonard Koppett publicized the theory. Since then, it's only been right about half the time. And even though there's no basis for a correlation between the winning team and stock market direction, it goes to show that indicators work until the herd takes notice and everyone changes their behavior in an effort to exploit the indicator.

The tendency of herd behavior to eliminate the benefit of an observed stock market pattern is quite simple. If the herd knows that a stock will increase in price tomorrow, their behavior will make the stock increase today. But if the stock already increased today, then it's too late to profit from this knowledge. Such is the impact of herd behavior.

When an investor publishes a book on market timing strategies that promises to make the reader rich, the investor better hope to profit handsomely from the book. Because the very act of other investors reading the book and implementing the strategies will reduce their impact.

Some argue that the January effect is still noticeable today. And it is, though it's more noticeable in some years than in others. That means it's risky, because there's no consistency. If you go back to 1942 when investment banker Sidney Wachtel first brought attention to the effect, it was much larger. A lot of money could be made from trading against the crowd. More and more people started doing it. And now you can't make very much money, if any, from betting on the January effect.

*So when is the best time to buy stocks? Is it in December? Or should we wait until January?* The answer is *yes!* And also *yes!* And if you can think of ten more months that might be considered opportune times to invest, the answer will consistently be *yes!*

New investors often make the mistake of thinking that investing is all about finding a cheap stock to get into at the right time, waiting for it to increase in value, and then identifying the right time to sell. In other words, they think it's about finding the tops and bottoms. It's not. In fact, that type of approach is incredibly dangerous. I admire the investor who can consistently pull off such a feat, but in all honesty, I have yet to meet her. My experience has been that investors who adopt this type of approach will either lose money or their portfolio will lag the market. Academic studies have shown that the more an investor trades, the worse they perform. This is partly due to additional commissions and taxes incurred through frequent trading, but also due to the fact that not every trade is the right trade.

The buy and hold approach is perceived as boring, but it works. It doesn't matter that the financial media devotes its time to individual stocks and regurgitating the opinions of large financial institutions. A smart investor understands that it's not wise to trade on the news, simply because the news is not a leading indicator. It will never tell you where the market is going next. Instead, the news provides commentary on events that caused the market to do what it just did.

I don't recommend relying on the news to determine a good entry point. Economic indicators can be more reliable. But the market is not static, and an indicator that worked in the past might not work in the future. If anything, economic indicators are a good metric for determining when to throw extra money at the market. We'll discuss this approach in more detail in the following chapter, but when it comes to entering the market with your monthly savings, the approach I use is not only effective, but incredibly easy to implement. It's called dollar cost averaging. And it's nothing more than the practice of placing the same amount of money on the stock market each month regardless what the market is doing. By investing the same amount each month, an investor can systematically average into a "below-average" price. There's no judgment involved, and you don't need to predict market direction. You simply average into a lucrative price over time because you are able to acquire more shares for the same amount of money when markets are down (rather than up). This is the starting place for our strategy, and we'll continue to dollar cost average right up until retirement.

But we don't want to dollar cost average into just the stock market. There's no protection against a crash if all we own are stocks. So instead, we want to diversify across different markets that don't always behave the same way in different economic environments. It provides a sense of safety. When one market starts going down, another might be going up, or moving sideways, or doing any number of things. I can't predict market direction, and most successful investors acknowledge that they can't either. Remember, there's only one Warren Buffett and there's only one Peter Lynch. Just about any other investor who brags about timing the market is bragging about the good times and declining to discuss the bad times. Or they're incredibly lucky.

In my opinion, investors place too much emphasis on trying to beat the market. We have both the media and the mutual fund industry to blame for the misconception that trying to beat the market is what investing is all about. They sell excitement, but they also sell risk. We have markets at our disposal that have always beaten inflation when invested in for the long-haul. And the instruments used to invest in these markets are incredibly cheap. Most passively managed index funds have incredibly small expense ratios. And if you purchase them through a discount broker, the commission is negligible.

You won't beat the market with an index fund, but you'll keep pace with the market, and that's all you need to do in order to earn a nice return. When you account for the savings incurred by avoiding the excess fees, taxes, and commissions that a trader will incur, the chances of consistently performing better than investors who try to beat the market are actually stacked in favor of the index fund holder.

The easiest markets to gain broad exposure to with index funds are the stock, bond, and real estate markets. You can hold entire markets if you choose, or gain exposure to specific sectors within each market. You can even branch off into foreign markets, hone in on emerging markets, or buy indexes that track stable blue chip stocks. The options are almost limitless, but it's important to understand what market segments you're exposed to, the risk involved with each segment, and the safety you build by combining markets that won't always move in tandem.

Stocks and real estate are going to provide the largest long-term gains. These are our equity markets. Young investors should be heavily weighted in favor of equities. As you progress towards retirement, you'll want to gradually reduce your exposure to equities as you increase your exposure to bonds. By the time you're rich, the bond market will provide the safety you desire (*whether or not it provides the yield you're after is a different story . . . and we'll discuss this issue in due course*).

The great thing about these markets is that they all pay a distribution in one form or another. Stocks pay dividends, bonds pay interest, and real estate pays rents. But the difference between each type of distribution is only important when it comes to taxes. And taxes do make a difference. You should always understand the tax implications before you make an investment. But that doesn't mean taxes come first. Our strategy is built on proper diversification combined with reinvested dividends. We're not going to sacrifice a sound investment strategy in order to minimize our tax liability. Instead, we're going to implement a strategy that provides the highest returns possible for our given tolerance for risk, and treat tax implications as a secondary concern.

Nobody likes to pay taxes, but it goes hand-in-hand with making money. And we're going to learn how to turn money into more money. Once the foundation has been implemented, taxes should be given the attention they deserve, and where possible, we should strive to reduce them.

A fourth asset class that deserves our attention is commodities. Generally, these aren't buy-and-hold investments. Most investors purchase commodities through contracts (or maybe an ETF that holds contracts on the commodity). Futures contracts are used to hedge the impact of price changes on a commodity that you either produce or need to purchase in the future. A farmer who is just starting to grow corn might enter into a futures contract with a chain of grocery stores. The contract will lock in a price at the time of signing, but the actual sale of corn will take place down the line. The farmer is then protected in the event that the market price for corn depreciates between signing and delivery. The chain of grocery stores is similarly protected in the event that the market price for corn appreciates between signing and delivery.

In its simplest form, this is why futures contracts exist. They provide protection to both parties. Another important feature of futures contracts is that they make pricing transparent. While traditional buying and selling might take place at an open market, futures contracts are bought and sold on an exchange. Information that is known about a commodity and events that have an impact on its price in the future will be factored into the futures contract. Everyone can see it, and it keeps markets efficient. But in today's online investing world, the futures contract has become a tool for short-term speculation. And if you don't sell the contract in time, you might actually have to deliver the commodity.

Commodities that appeal to long-term investors are few in number. Corn has a shelf life. Same with live stock. Even oil, which sits on the throne of being the most useful commodity in existence, goes bad after five years. But gold and other precious metals last forever. In fact, the De Beers family has invested extensively in advertising campaigns aimed at promoting the fact that diamonds are forever. They did so in an effort to eliminate the secondary market for previously owned diamonds, and their campaign has been tremendously successful.

We aren't going to invest too heavily in commodities and we're not going to trade futures contracts. We'll leave that to the speculators. Instead, we might consider buying an ETF that holds gold, and perhaps a second one that holds silver. And we'll use these to hedge the probability that at some point in time, equities are going to tank.

Gold and other precious metals are interesting commodities to invest in, and there are three incredibly strong reasons why. First, they have an inverse relationship to the dollar. This makes sense, because the dollar was at one time tied to gold. In other words, our currency used to be worth its weight in gold. But ever since we've been on a fiat currency, the Treasury has been at liberty to print as many dollars as it wants, all while the gold supply remains relatively constant. As a result, the spending power of our currency declines, but gold continues to hold its weight. When inflation sets in, there are all sorts of investments that appreciate in price, while money left in a checking account will depreciate. Gold won't necessarily appreciate in accordance to the rate of inflation, but when an economic catastrophe occurs, the value of gold is re-measured, and those invested in it prosper while everyone else watches their portfolio take a hit.

The second reason that makes precious metals a unique investment opportunity is that they can't go bankrupt. Just like a currency is subject to depreciate, so is a business. And if a business isn't run efficiently (or simply provides a product or service that is no longer in demand), that business can go bankrupt. It can be liquidated, and shareholders are lucky if there's any salvage value left for them after the lawyers are done collecting their fees. Unlike a publicly traded company or real estate investment trust, precious metals cannot go bankrupt. We can diversify away the risk of a specific company going out of business by holding the greater market. And that's exactly what we're going to do. But once this is done, we need to diversify away the likelihood of the entire market taking a hit. In order to do that, we need to invest in multiple markets. Gold and other precious metals provide an opportunity to diversify across markets, and this leads to the third reason that makes gold and other precious metals such unique investments.

The investment cycle of precious metals is known to move against that of equities. In other words, when stocks and real estate are doing well, gold and other precious metals are likely to be in the dumps. But when equities make a move for the worst, gold and other precious metals start to rally. Given that the typical bull market outlasts the average bear market by greater than 3 years, we can expect gold and other precious metals to spend more time in the dumps than they spend going up. But when it's time for gold and other precious metals to rally, they rally hard.

In fact, a stock market crash shouldn't really be viewed as a destruction of wealth. Rather, it's a transfer of wealth. Those invested in stocks take a huge hit while those invested in gold and other precious metals thrive. Or, if you have a thoroughly diversified portfolio, the act of rebalancing will force you to perpetually sell more and more gold as the price skyrockets, and subsequently reinvest the proceeds in equities while they're priced at a discount.

I recommend allocating no more than 10% of the portfolio to precious metals, and go ahead and hope that you lose money on it. If you do, it means your stock and real estate investments are paying off. But when equity markets are getting trampled, that 10% is likely to shoot for the stars, and through the act of rebalancing you'll reap the rewards in a systematic fashion that doesn't require you to predict future events. Just let the markets work through their cycles and bring the gains to you.

The biggest downside to investing in precious metals is that they don't pay any form of dividend. There's no passive income to be earned. This is an investment that you hold purely for capital appreciation. So again, limit your holdings to 10%. The strategy that we're going to implement is a long-term strategy, and we don't want to lose decades of building our dividend income into more and more shares. But when other markets tank and precious metals shine, you'll be glad that a portion of your portfolio is invested in them.

When it comes to long-term strategies, gold is the portfolio addition that delivers the type of hedge we're interested in. It moves through long-term secular cycles, and it isn't highly correlated to the other asset classes we'll be investing in. If we're going to invest in a commodity, we want one where the price reacts to economic events rather than the coming weather forecast. We want investor behavior to have as small an impact as possible.

The only scenario I can envision where long-term stock market or real estate returns do not beat inflation would be if investors quit investing in these markets altogether. I hope we're all in agreement that the chances of this happening are incredibly slim. It's far more likely that a pool of investors will stop investing for short durations of time. When they do, it's called a crash. But this type of behavior has never persisted. When stocks or real estate are selling at really cheap prices, investors eventually get back in. The smart money understands that the best time to buy stocks or real estate is when they're performing poorly. This not only moves the market higher, put serves as an integral step in the market cycle. It's the process of allowing different markets to work through their cycles that brings us returns, more so than if we simply bought into one market for the long-haul. A properly diversified investor should have confidence in a long-term approach. The bottoms create buying opportunities, and the tops create selling opportunities. If we're invested in markets that don't exhibit strong positive correlation—that is, they don't move up and down in complete unison—then we're in a good position to automatically buy low and sell high through the process of rebalancing our portfolio.

Granted, we only want to invest in markets that are going to move higher with time. Gold isn't going to move in unison with our bond and equity holdings, but over time, we want all of our investments to not only move higher, but to also beat inflation. If we can't expect these types of long-term results from a market, then we shouldn't be investing in it. But even with markets that can be expected to move higher with time, we can't expect them to do so in a straight line. They ebb and flow. There are going to be bumps in the road, and we'll encounter a crash or two along the way. We'll also experience market conditions where everything keeps going higher and higher for no apparent reason. And there will be times when it's apparent that certain markets don't know what they want to do. It all sounds very chaotic, but we can improve our performance by structuring the portfolio in such a way that volatility creates opportunities. Instead of chasing after a market that shows signs of momentum, we're going to sit back and let momentum in certain markets, combined with temporary-depreciation in other markets, bring the gains to us. And we don't have to worry about herd mentality overriding the impact, so long as we stick to a pre-determined schedule.

It all comes down to rebalancing. We're going to structure the portfolio in accordance to the amount of risk we're willing to assume, and we'll use bonds as an anchor to keep the portfolio safe. With time, the percent of the portfolio that's allocated to both bonds and our other asset classes will change. Real estate might edge upwards. Stocks could take a dive. Gold will perform well when the economy is suffering. And we anticipate that our bonds, on average, are just going to mosey along as they pay a bit of interest. But maybe something completely different will happen. *We don't know!* But by combining different assets in proportions that align with our tolerance for risk, we prepare ourselves to increase the size of our portfolio based on these movements.

It's important to understand that the primary objective of rebalancing is to maintain desired weights. As the name implies, we want to keep the portfolio in balance. It keeps the tolerated level of risk in check. But what forces us to rebalance is the act of some assets moving higher as others move lower. So in order to get things back on track, we need to sell assets that have appreciated in value (for a gain) and buy assets that have depreciated in value (at a discount). As the markets move through their cycles, we eventually sell the discount purchases at a gain as we buy more of the previous winners, but this time at a discount.

That's what a strong portfolio is designed to do. It follows long-term trends and systematically brings profits to the investor. But we're also going to profit from short-term movements, albeit in smaller increments.

Some investors chase after huge returns by moving large chunks of capital from one asset class to another, all based on what they think the markets are going to do next. In other words, they're trying to time the market. That's not the approach we're going to take. We prefer safety and surety over an opportunity to snatch a large reward by putting large sums of money at risk. All we have to do is rebalance the portfolio. It forces us to systematically skim some gains off the top in order to reinvest in a different market that's priced at a discount.

As we'll see in *Chapter 7: Rebalancing*, this doesn't require much effort, and there's absolutely no fortune telling involved. We don't need a crystal ball to be successful. We're simply going to settle in on a risk tolerance that we're comfortable with, and then allow markets to do whatever it is they're going to do next. That's all there is to it. And we'll be better off if we don't try anything fancy along the way.

What makes rebalancing such a reliable tool is that investor behavior can't override the impact. With a market timing strategy like the January effect, the herd reacts in unison, all buying and selling at the same time in an effort to reap the same rewards. And it doesn't work—*at least not for long*. A rebalancing approach is different because investors don't all rebalance at the same time. Some only rebalance once a year. Others rebalance semiannually or quarterly.

Even if many, many investors rebalance with the same frequency, their schedules are going to be completely different. If you rebalance on an annual basis, there are 12 different months to choose from. Semiannual rebalancers have six different pairs of months to choose from, and quarterly rebalancers have four different combinations at their disposal. On top of that, not every investor rebalances based on the passing of time. Some investors rebalance based on the size of a departure from their desired asset allocation. For example, some investors might rebalance every time their bond allocation strays plus or minus 5% from the desired weight. Others might not rebalance until its moved 7.5% from the desired weight.

There are literally millions of investors practicing this approach, but they don't succumb to herd mentality because there's no driving factor that forces everyone to adopt the same rebalancing schedule. This allows investors to reap rewards without having to predict the behavior of the herd.

It's important to understand herd mentality. It drives many short-term market movements. But it's even more important to understand that our strategy works in light of herd mentality, because it relies predominantly on long-term market movements. Let the herd do as it pleases. We're going to play a safer game, and our returns will be more consistent as a result.

When you're done with *Preparing For Financial Success,* you'll be able to implement the strategy with confidence. The plan works as long as you see things through, and that means sticking it out through both thick and thin. It's fun to invest when everything keeps going up. But downturns serve a purpose too, and it's the long-term investor who's in a position to benefit from such occurrences.

Once the plan is implemented, it must be followed. But I don't just want to focus on implementation. I also want to discuss theory. I want every reader to understand where the principals come from and why they work. It's through such an understanding that investors gain the confidence to persevere through the most bearish of market conditions. It never pays to abandon ship when the stock market takes a turn for the worst. See it through. In the long run, your portfolio will be bigger than it would be had the stock market never tanked. That's the beauty of an approach that systematically forces you to buy low and sell high. You'll capture some great discounts when everyone else gets scared and sells. And there's no guesswork involved.

I hope you found the overview of our investment strategy digestible. And I hope you're excited about implementing a strategy that systematically delivers gains without requiring you to make predictions. But if you feel like you need further clarification, that's fine. We have a separate chapter dedicated to each of the steps we'll be implementing. In fact, we've already discussed the first two steps: setting a goal and budgeting for that goal. Now that we have some savings set aside, *it's time to invest!*

The next step is dollar cost averaging. I've provided an overview. Now let's have a closer look at why it works so well.

# Chapter 4

## Use a Boring Entry Point to Buy Boring Investments . . . *And Come Out Ahead!*

So we have money to invest and we want to get the best return possible with that money. But we're just starting out and we don't have a whole lot of experience, so we need some guidance. Thankfully, we have friends who invest. They know all about it. We can tell because they're always talking about an exciting new tech company, some pharmaceutical company that's on the verge of a major breakthrough, or how much money they're going to make once the cannabis industry undergoes further deregulation. It's always something interesting and they're always on top of the next big thing. It's even more reassuring when they talk about a stock they just sold. Their gains are locked in and they just made a massive amount of money in a really short period of time. *And now we want in on the action!* But we're not going to jump in headfirst and follow our friends down this path of excitement. Instead, we're going to start by managing our expectations.

It's important to understand that our friends only brag about their conquests. They failed to mention that the big gain they just recognized almost offsets the losses they incurred last January. And that "next big thing" that they've invested in? *In all likelihood, it won't be.* Even if you never recall the name of the company, you'll know it didn't turn into the next big thing because your friends will continue to get out of bed every morning and go to work.

There's lots of excitement in the stock market. And I can't deny that I occasionally get an itch for a piece of the action. But there's a difference between dedicating your retirement savings to the action and having a separate pool of funds that you invest less discriminately.

When your friends talk about that up and coming tech company they've invested in, how much do you think they've invested? Do they have all of their investments allocated across companies that promise to be the next big thing? Or are most of their funds invested conservatively, and when they talk about the action, they're only talking about a small percent of their holdings?

If you want to secure a safe finish, then the overwhelming majority of your portfolio should be invested in assets that are just downright boring. That's the safest way to go. We're going to buy funds that no one would ever care to discuss at a cocktail party. It won't be a quick path to riches, but it won't wreck our portfolios either.

If you get an itch for some action, satisfy the itch with funds that aren't dedicated to your retirement. You might even build an allocation into the budget we discussed in chapter two. If you're setting aside money to trade stocks, which is fundamentally different from investing, it should come from the 30% of your take home pay that gets allocated to wants. Trading stocks is a hobby. It's not a need and it's not what your retirement savings is for. Sure, it can be a fun and rewarding hobby . . . *at times!* But it needs to be treated as separate and distinct from your savings. You should always allocate *at least* 20% of your take home pay to retirement savings. And you'll want to keep your retirement savings in an account that's completely separate from where you do your trading. *Why?* Because when our friends identify the next big tech company, or some pharmaceutical company that's destined to cure cancer, or that cannabinoid company that's going to cure everyone's pain and suffering, we might not have any funds to invest. It's possible that our discretionary funds will already be exhausted, but we have this stream of dividend income that keeps building up in our retirement account. *Don't speculate with the dividend income.* Part of our strategy for building a plentiful retirement is to reinvest the dividends. We're going to reinvest them in boring index funds that will pay additional dividends for us to reinvest in yet more boring index funds, and so on and so forth.

It's wise to keep funds separate. If you practice more than one investment style, keep the funds separate. If you're investing for different reasons, keep the funds separate. To build a retirement, you need a certain level of savings, but you also need to invest the savings according to your objective. How much longer is your investment horizon? And how safe do the funds need to be? These are the questions that dictate how your retirement savings should be invested. And that's what *Preparing For Financial Success* is all about. If you make other investments for a different purpose, keep them in a separate account. It helps keep you focused on your strategy, and it helps ensure that you only invest your retirement savings in the most boring manner possible.

To me, retirement investing is not a trading game—*it's a building game.* Instead of moving in and out of stocks that promise excitement while exposing us to risk, we're going to invest in index funds that provide broad market exposure. And we're going to reinvest our dividends each and every step of the way. In other words, we're going to build, and we have a variety of asset classes at our disposal to build upon.

We'll buy at least one fund that tracks the stock market. We'll do the same for real estate, and the same for bonds. And as we discussed above, we might even buy an ETF that invests in gold. *And that's it! Nice and boring!*

But we're not going to stop boring ourselves here. Choosing our investments is only the first step. Now we have to find an entry point. Markets are volatile, and a lot of investors analyze volatility in an effort to get in at the most lucrative point. There are two primary ways to go about this. You can select your investment and then attempt to buy it on a dip, or you can keep money on the sideline, eager to throw it all in during the next market crash. We're not going to take either of these approaches. Instead, we'll buy in at the same time every month. It's nice and boring. And we'll see shortly why it works to our advantage.

## Random Walk Defined

I'm not a proponent of market timing. Instead, I subscribe to the random walk theory. This was popularized by Burton G Malkiel in his 1973 classic, *A Random Walk Down Wall Street.* The premise is just as the title indicates. The movement of stocks is completely random and unpredictable. The investor cannot gain an edge by waiting for an advantageous entry point because the stock is just as likely to move up as it is to move down . . . *or maybe sideways.* I really don't know, and neither does Mr. Malkiel. Hence the term *random*.

Simply stated, every stock movement is independent of all other movements. The fact that a stock went up yesterday—or maybe it went down, or even sideways—tells us absolutely nothing about what it's going to do tomorrow. The movements are truly independent. If a basketball player makes a free throw, it has no impact on the probability of him making the next free throw. If you flip a coin and it comes up heads, it has no impact on the likelihood of the next flip coming up heads. This is the nature of "random," and it applies to stock prices just the same as it applies to coin flipping and free throws. And the investment world knows this because Mr. Malkiel articulates it so well.

The book is a fascinating read that begins with a history lesson on tulip mania and the South Sea bubble, and then discusses the nature of randomness in the stock market, which is no different from the randomness encountered when throwing darts at a list of stocks. It ends with a rationalization that investors are better off investing in index funds over individual stocks.

There are many followers to this approach. Now in its 12th edition, the book has sold over 1.5 million copies. I mentioned above, it's an extremely easy—*and boring*—approach to follow. But it takes some experience in the market before the typical investor becomes a random walker.

The approach I use can be taught in a very short amount of time. It only takes 30 minutes. What can't be taught in a short amount of time is why all those other approaches that our friends keep talking about aren't very good ideas. The true hardship of becoming a successful investor is learning why all those other methods that seem to promise big returns can't be relied on. It's something most of us learn through experience. Some learn the lesson quicker than others, and some learn the lesson with smaller losses than others. It's the investor who gets lucky his first time out that is most likely to become overconfident and keep going at it until the losses become overwhelming. It's no different from beating the house on your first trip to the casino . . . *and then thinking that you can do it again and again*. But when it comes to investing, it's extremely easy to implement an approach that stacks long-term odds in your favor. When it comes to casinos, the long-term odds are stacked in the house's favor.

As an investor, if you see things through during the bad times and continue to reinvest your dividends no matter what you think the market might do next, then the odds are stacked in your favor. Your portfolio will increase in value and your long-term results will exceed the rate of inflation.

**My Confession**

With regard to market timing, I do have one confession to make. I'm a casual fan of predicting market bottoms. It's a guilty pleasure, more or less. When markets are doing well, it's incredibly difficult to call a top. The herd can just keep pushing prices higher and higher, and it's incredibly difficult to predict when exactly the herd will get scared and change directions. But when markets crash, it's really easy to identify securities that are grossly underpriced. And that makes for a lucrative opportunity to throw some *extra* money at the market.

I emphasize the word *extra* because extra is exactly what it should be. When markets perform poorly, it's time to consider investing extra money. Maybe cut down on our wants for a few months. In the short run, we can't switch to a smaller house, but we can take a break from the Starbucks just as easily as we can forgo eating out for a season (*or two*). And we can postpone that vacation to the Bahamas we were about to book.

Investing *more* when markets are down makes sense. But the last thing we want to do is leave our retirement savings on the sideline waiting for the next crash. We're likely to miss out on some pretty nice returns if we do. We have no idea how high a market will go before it crashes. Even when a market is noticeably overpriced, it can keep going higher and higher. The herd isn't always rational. In fact, investors can be quite greedy, and they'll chase after momentum for however long they can. Perhaps they're relying on a greater fool to pay even more for the security that they just bought at an inflated price, or maybe they just don't understand how markets work. The investing world attracts all types. The best we can do is accept that it's difficult to predict a market top and implement a strategy that doesn't require us to make such predictions.

When it comes to predicting market bottoms, it's easier to implement a systematic approach. A market can go up indefinitely, but it can only go down as far as zero. I don't actually expect the markets we're investing in to do that (though there's no guarantee that at some point in the future they won't come close). What I do expect is to get really good deals when markets trade below their moving averages. And I expect to get even better deals when markets are in full-blown bear territory. I don't have to time it exactly; I just need to see things through once I've made my investment.

But again, when it comes to predicting market bottoms, we're talking about throwing *extra* money at the market. We're not going to stop making investments until this happens. In just a bit we'll discuss why. But first, let's discuss the entry points that we'll use regardless of what the market is doing.

**So how do we know when to buy?**

We need an entry point. And while we might prefer an entry point when markets are down, that won't always be the case. When it comes to our fixed monthly contributions, we don't want to wait for a better entry point, because there's no guarantee that one will come along anytime soon. But even more important, our entry point isn't based on what the herd is doing. If other investors want to sell their holdings and stash the money under their beds, that's fine. If they have delusions that the market is never going to crash, that's fine too.

When our friends talk about their conquests in the stock market, they're not just talking about how they identified the next big thing. They're also talking about how good they are at plotting graphs and interpreting patterns. They understand herd mentality. They can predict whether or not the January effect will be in season this year. That's what they keep telling us. And it doesn't matter if it doesn't pan out, because when these things don't happen, they've already discovered a more lucrative pattern. It makes little difference if they're on their first glass of pinot or their third. They know how to find the right entry point to the stock market, and they're not bashful about sharing this.

We're happy that our friends can proclaim such success. But we're on a different route. Our entry point is going to be very, very boring. We're going to buy in at the same time every month. It will most likely be right after we get paid. A portion of our paycheck might even be direct deposited into our brokerage account. Or we might have to wait for a transfer to clear. But whatever the process, the same amount of money will hit our brokerage account at roughly the same time every month, and that's when we're going to make our next investment. It's nice and boring. But the great thing is, we'll achieve above average results because of it.

The process is called dollar cost averaging. It's really easy. We simply place the same amount of money into the same investments each month. *What could be more boring than that?* We'll earn some dividend income along the way. So we'll go ahead and reinvest however much we've accrued at the same time that we make each of our predetermined investments.

We have confidence that our investments will work in our favor over the long haul, even when short-term movements *seem* to work against us. In actuality, the short-term movements also work to our advantage, so long as we don't try to predict them. It's all about buying low and selling high. We're going to implement a rebalancing strategy that forces us to do so in a very systematic manner. The end result is a portfolio that continually grows.

I hope this sounds simple because it is. And if it doesn't sound simple, it should by the time we're finished *Chapter 8: Why it Works*.

**Dollar Cost Averaging Dissected**

By investing the same amount each month, an investor can systematically average into a "below-average" price. That's the magic of our approach. There's no guesswork involved.

Let's assume we buy an index fund that holds the entire stock market. For simplicity, we'll assume that the fund costs $20 per share and the monthly investment will be $500. This affords us 25 shares. If during the next month the fund takes a big dip and sells for only $15 per share, then the second investment of $500 affords us 33 shares. But here's the kicker, the average price paid per share is less than the average of $20 and $15. In other words, we've secured an average investment price that is less than the average of what the security was priced at when the investments were made.

Let's have a look from a mathematical standpoint:

We bought shares at $20 and $15, and the average of these two amounts is $17.50.

(20 + 15) / 2 = 17.50

However, the fact that $500 bought more shares at $15 than it did at $20 means that the average price paid per share is only $17.25.

500 / 20 = 25

500 / 15 = 33

25 + 33 = 58

1,000 / 58 = 17.25

That's the power of dollar cost averaging. Over time, we will continue to make monthly investments of $500, but the average price paid for the fund will be less than the average price that the fund has sold for, simply because more shares are purchased when the fund drops in price.

The beauty of this approach is that it allows us to accumulate wealth without having to predict market direction. We don't have to worry about whether or not *now* is the appropriate time to buy. The answer will always be a resounding *yes!*

As time passes, the impact progressively grows more profound. We're only investing in markets that we expect to beat inflation over a course of 10 to 20 years. But short-term movements create opportunities to get in during a dip. Again, we're not going to wait for the dips, because stock movements are perceived as random. We don't know if or when the dip is coming. The market could move higher and never return to where it stands today. It could take a dip and recover quickly, or it could take more than a dip and recover very, very slowly. Your guess is as good as mine. But if we continue to dollar cost average for 20, 30, or even 40 years, we're going to catch our fair share of dips without even trying. We'll also catch some bumps, but again, that's fine, because we acquire more shares during the dips than we do during the bumps, which allows us to average into a lucrative price.

After a prolonged period of time, we have two distinct advantages working in our favor: (1) we've invested in markets that perform well, so we should expect our investments to appreciate regardless of our exact entry point, and (2) we've acquired more shares per amount invested when markets take a hit, which brings down the average cost of our investment. Now factor in the likelihood of experiencing multiple bear markets during a 30-year investment span, and think about what this does to the average cost of our investments.

Yes, we want markets that will increase in value. But we're actually better off if they don't move up in a straight line. The dips are our friends. We'll see in *Chapter 7: Rebalancing* that they provide benefits that are even better than what we've discussed so far.
In just a couple chapters, we're going to discuss the benefits of reinvesting our dividends, a process known as compounding. Just like our monthly contribution, we'll want to invest them systematically. There's no point in waiting for a lucrative entry point because there's no way to consistently predict which direction the market will move next. From a dollar cost averaging perspective, earning a dividend simply means that you have more to invest. When you throw your monthly savings into the portfolio, go ahead and reinvest your dividend income along with it. The same principles apply. It's better to reinvest dividends when markets are down, just as it's better to invest savings when markets are down. But there's another distinct advantage that comes with investing in markets that pay a dividend. Not only do you accumulate more shares when markets are down, but you also get better dividend yields. That's because dividend yield has an inverse relationship to the price of the stock. When

the price of a stock drops, the yield goes up. It won't do you much good if you already own the stock. But when making new investments, a higher yield means all the difference in the world. And you'll continue to reap the rewards for however long you hold the investment.

**Reversion to the Mean**

Our strategy is based on investments in index funds that provide broad market exposure. That's the safest road we can take. We're not looking to beat markets (because every attempt we take at beating the market increases the likelihood that we'll lag the market). We won't be relying on individual stock. But that doesn't mean we can't benefit from learning the approaches that a stock trader implements. Reversion to the mean is a prime example.

Reversion to the mean suggests that if a stock's current selling price differs significantly from its historic average, the price will eventually move back in the direction of the historic average. A stock that has been moving up (or down) is expected to revert at some point. And while it cannot be guaranteed with certainty when this reversion will occur, the herd behaves in such a way that patterns are formed.

The 200-day moving average is a metric commonly used to measure a stock's current price in relation to its average price over the past 200 days. As the name implies, the average will change each day because it's a moving average, and this keeps the figure relevant. If a stock is priced too far above its 200-day moving average, we assume that the price will eventually drop. If a stock is priced too far below its 200-day moving average, we assume that the price will eventually rise. Our goal is not to make a quick profit off of this reversion. Rather, we're going to review a variety of attributes for each investment we consider. If we find a good candidate for a long-term investment, we'll buy it. But all else being equal, it's better to invest in a stock while it's priced below its 200-day moving average than to get in on a stock that's priced above its 200-day moving average. If two stocks are equally attractive, then it's best to purchase the stock that appears most underpriced in relation to its 200-day moving average.

When a stock drops too far below its moving average, a resistance point will form as the herd takes notice and traders buy up the stock. When a stock advances too high above its moving average, a resistance point will also form, this time as traders take their gains. These are nothing more than short-term movements influenced by investor behavior. The long-term trend is contingent on the performance of the company, as it should be.

The view that a stock price will revert to its mean, of course, contradicts the notion that stock movements are random. And that's okay. Even though a herd mentality can be observed, the herd is easier to document after the movements have been made. Just because the herd is moving in a certain direction, it doesn't mean a news release won't come along and force the herd to change its path. This happens quite frequently, and it supports the notion of a random walk.

As index fund investors, we care about reversion to the mean because it indicates whether or not investments are fairly priced. The concept is used to trade stocks, but can easily be applied to index funds. And while we're going to dollar cost average no matter what, we understand that a fund is a better buy—and we accumulate more shares—when it is priced below its moving average.

Knowing this, it's possible to add variations to our dollar cost averaging approach that will further improve our long-term performance. The best time to throw extra money at the market is when markets are down. This notion can be combined with a dollar cost averaging approach. And while I'd love to take credit for the concept, *I can't.* I can only take credit for sharing the concept with you . . . that is, unless you've already read *Yes, You Can Time The Market!* by Ben Stein and Phil DeMuth.

**Stein and DeMuth**

While it's fun to watch our investments appreciate in value, we know that the investments made during downturns are destined to appreciate the most. They reduce the average cost of our holdings and pave the way for superior long-term returns.

Market timing is often viewed as synonymous with short-term trading, but the far-sighted investor who has the patience to implement a long-term market timing approach is going to reap some rewards. Ben Stein and Phil DeMuth advocate such an approach. In the above mentioned book, they review 100 years of stock market returns in order to devise a systematic long-term market-timing approach. And while the book is fascinating, the approach is completely boring . . . *so right off the bat we know it's worthy of our attention!*

The approach is more or less a variation of dollar cost averaging that keeps an eye on moving averages and anticipates that prices will revert to the mean. Of course, the 200-day moving average becomes a meaningless gauge when focusing on long-term results, so Stein and DeMuth rely on a 15-year moving average for their analysis. They ask the question, *what happens if we only buy stocks when the market is priced below its 15-year moving average?*

Relying on 100 years of historic data, they conclude that investors can dramatically increase their long-term returns by only dollar cost averaging into stocks when the market is priced below its 15-year moving average. When the market is priced above its 15-year moving average, funds should be held in a money market account until things change.

Returning to the above example where the investor placed $500 on the stock market each month regardless of price, the Stein and DeMuth variation would be to place the $500 in a money market account when the market is priced above its 15-year moving average, and then invest $1,000 each month that the market is priced below its 15-year moving average. This plays on the notion that dollar cost averaging forces the investor to acquire more shares when markets are down, but magnifies the effect by using the 15-year moving average to time entry points.

Through analysis of the historic data, Stein and DeMuth develop predictions of what, on average, will happen if this approach is followed for 5, 10, 15, and 20-year periods. At five years, the moving-average-conscious investor is likely to perform comparable to the traditional dollar cost averaging investor. But as longer timespans are analyzed, Stein and

DeMuth show that there is an advantage to making investments only when markets are priced below their moving average. In fact, there's a strong *possibility* that the moving-average-conscious investor will accrue returns that are more than double the size of those earned through traditional dollar cost averaging, should they stick with the approach for 20 years.

I emphasize the word "*possibility*" because the study is based on historic data. Yes, 100 years is a statistically significant period, but it doesn't change the fact that past performance is not a guarantee of future performance. And when you implement a 20-year strategy, it's really important that you get it right the first time through, because it might take an extra 20 years to get things back on track.

While I admire this approach, I find it hard to implement, especially given that the past 10 years have provided very few buying opportunities. A prolonged bull run that follows a crash will keep the market above its moving average for a significant period of time. Given that interest rates have been kept artificially low in an effort to keep the economy elevated, the funds wouldn't have earned very much in a money market account.

Developing an investment style is a matter of personal preference. I feel more comfortable implementing a traditional dollar cost averaging approach. When markets keep going higher, there's a fear of missing out. Investors succumb to it all the time. It's the very reason why it's easier to pick a bottom than a top. Those who follow the Stein and DeMuth approach might question if they're truly on the right path, or if they are just letting a series of acceptable buy-in opportunities pass them buy. During a 10-year bull run, this would be an easy question to ask. And the true danger is that we might change our approach at the wrong time and buy in just before the market tanks. It's happened to investors before and it will happen to investors again.

Another downside to the Stein and DeMuth approach is that it's subject to herd mentality. We know that traditional dollar cost averaging doesn't create a herd because investors dollar cost average on different schedules. But if too many investors follow the Stein and DeMuth approach, a herd could form. What would happen if the herd only made new investments when the stock market is priced below its 15-year moving average? For starters, it wouldn't stay below the 15-year moving average for long, because the herd would start buying mass quantities as soon as it does. This could conceivably create a sideways market where the herd buys during very short dips, pushes it back up, and then lets it dip again. *How long would this last?* Who knows, because the herd always changes course once a pattern is formed. But I'm sure a host of other repercussions would follow, and this would naturally force the herd to react yet again.

Fortunately, I don't think we have to worry about the Stein and DeMuth approach succumbing to herd mentality, mainly because Wall Street won't acknowledge it. Financial advisors love dollar cost averaging because it provides steady commissions. It's only investors who have read Stein and DeMuth's work that are able to benefit from the knowledge. Whether they implement the strategy as discussed or rely on a variation where they increase the size of the investments when markets trend lower, they should continue to see strong long-term results because the herd hasn't stumbled upon the approach. Yes, there are plenty of investors who understand that the best time to buy is when the market is low, but the systematic approach the Stein and DeMuth have developed is quite extraordinary. There's much that can be learned and borrowed from this approach, yet I'm still hesitant to implement it in its entirety.

I prefer the traditional dollar cost averaging approach. I find it comforting in both up and down markets. I never suffer from the fear of missing out. And it better lends itself to the rebalancing strategy that we'll discuss in *Chapter 7: Rebalancing*. But that doesn't mean I'm going to dismiss the Stein and DeMuth approach altogether. They make a compelling argument for market timing, and because of this, I'm always looking for ways to tighten my budget and toss a little extra into the portfolio when the stock market trends below its 15-year moving average. It's actions such as these that make the difference between a comfortable retirement and a more than comfortable retirement.

Wealth isn't destroyed when markets crash, *it's transferred.* Finding ways to increase the size of your investments when markets are down can make all the difference in the world. It's okay to have a little excitement along the way, and investing more than you normally would while others are selling is one of the safest ways to extract excitement from the market. Once you've had as much excitement as you can stomach, it's time to focus on something that's boring, like dividend income.

**Compounding Dividends**

Dividends are particularly boring, and right now, they're about as boring as they've ever been. That's because the

S&P 500 is yielding less than 2%. The return on your high interest checking account might even be higher than the average yield of your stock portfolio. That's why our friends don't care about dividends. If they get one, great. But they're chasing after gains, not waiting for their dividend income to come rolling in. They prefer young companies that are trying to do something new and revolutionary. In other words, they prefer companies that invest their profits in new projects instead of distributing them to the shareholders. From the company's perspective, there's nothing wrong with that.

There are many, many successful companies who have never paid a dividend. Amazon (AMZN), Facebook (FB), Alphabet Inc. (GOOG), and Twitter, Inc. (TWTR) all come to mind. In fact, companies with valuable digital real estate are currently the least likely to pay a dividend. And these are exciting companies.

Over the five-year period ended in the spring of 2019, Amazon (AMZN) increased in value by 555%. Facebook (FB) jumped 234% while Alphabet Inc. (GOOG) jumped 129%. And Twitter (TWTR) moseyed along with just a 24% increase over the course of five years—*and with no dividend distribution whatsoever.*

Our friends might own all five. They like their digital real estate. And our friends are also very young. In fact, they're so young that they weren't invested in the stock market during the dotcom bubble. They're not the least bit scared of a company like Amazon (AMZN), whose PE ratio currently rests at 80. Besides, if it wasn't such a good deal, people wouldn't pay so much for it.

With our approach, we'll benefit from these same companies, because they're included in our index funds. We'll get the growth when it's provided, we'll hold other assets that provide protection when stocks come back down to something reasonable (or even plummet to something way below reasonable), and we'll earn dividend income through both thick and thin. That's the benefit of broad market exposure. We simply hold an index that represents the entire stock market. By doing so, we get the companies who reinvest their earnings in new projects, along with companies that distribute their earnings to the shareholders. Today, dividend income on the S&P 500 (SPY) only averages out to 1.85%, but we'll take it. And we'll build it into something that's worth more than 1.85% of our investment, all because we'll reinvest it in assets that both pay dividends and increase in value.

We like dividends for two distinct reasons: (1) they can't be manipulated, and (2) they allow us to build.

Companies who don't distribute dividends, but instead reinvest their earnings in new projects, are evaluated by their net income (or earnings per share). This number can be manipulated. That's what Enron did. That's what WorldCom did. And that's what Bernard L. Madoff Investment Securities LLC did. Granted, the former wasn't a publicly traded company, but the impact was nonetheless the same: *numbers were manipulated and investors got burned.* It all comes down to the fact that these companies were evaluated on reported earnings, not the amount of cash they were able to routinely distribute for extended periods of time.

Dividends can't be manipulated. They're a cash outflow. In order for a company to pay a dividend, they need to come up with the cash. And a company with a history of increasing their dividend each year for an extended period of time, say 25 years or more, must have solid earnings. Otherwise, the well would have run dry many years ago.

I'm a huge fan of the ProShares S&P 500 Dividend Aristocrats ETF (NOBL). The fund holds every company from the S&P 500 that maintains a market cap of at least $3 billion and has also increased their dividend each year for at least the past 25 years. In order to do this, the earnings must be real. It's a sign of long-term strength.

These aren't the highest yielding stocks available. In many cases, the dividend payment from these companies is far from competitive, and that's fine. A company doesn't need to distribute all of their earnings. In fact, the dividend is considered more sustainable if they don't. And we like dividend payers that also have new projects to invest some of their earnings in. To an extent, the lighter the dividend, the more likely we are to get strong capital gains. The S&P 500 Dividend Aristocrats has representation from all 11 sectors of the S&P 500. This by itself doesn't make for a diversified portfolio, but it's a good start towards being well diversified within the stock market.

The second reason we like dividends is because of their functionality. *They allow us to build!* In other words, they compound. Dividends are paid on a per share basis. We can use those dividends to buy more shares, which in turn will pay additional dividends, and so on and so forth. The price of a stock will fluctuate. Some go up, some go down, and some take a hit from which they never return. The same is true of an index of stocks, except an index that provides broad market exposure is expected to always recover from a hit. That's why they make such good long-term investments.

The dividend investor is content to let their holdings fluctuate. It's not about what the investment is worth a year after you buy it, or even two to three years after you buy it. It's about what it's worth when you sell it, and all the dividends you receive in between.

If the portfolio is built around index funds, or even a prudently selected group of individual stocks, the income stream will be relatively consistent, and with this stream the dividend investor will build more streams. It's not about trading in and out of the right stocks at the right time. Dividend investors are content with the average capital gains provided by the market and their ability to build.

It all sounds very boring. But over 20, 30, or even 40 years, the process of reinvesting dividends can easily provide hundreds of thousands of dollars in additional capital. It's all contingent on how much you save and how prudently you invest. In fact, the dividend investor takes comfort in the boredom, because they know what happens when their friends chase a hot new stock and incur a loss.

Let's say that hot new biotech company your friends are chasing incurs a 10% drop immediately after you succumb to their advice and buy in. In order to break even, you now need an 11.11% gain. This might not sound quite right, but it is. Let's take a look at the math and see how this works:

You invest $1,000 just before the stock drops by 10%. So 90% of your invested capital remains.

1,000 x 90% = 900

You've lost $100. To break even, you need to earn your $100 back. But remember, you're now working with only $900, not $1,000.

100 / 900 = 11.11%

So in order to earn the money back, you need to find gains that, in percentage terms, are larger than the loss you just incurred. This gives us a third distinct reason why we like dividends: (3) they're always positive.

Gains have the potential to completely dwarf dividends. We just saw how Amazon (AMZN) increased 555% in five years. But sometimes stocks lose money, and it can take a lot longer to earn the money back than it took to lose it.

Dividends are small but consistently positive. When stocks decline in value, we still get a distribution. And the dividends we reinvest when stocks are down benefit us more than the dividends we reinvest when stocks are up. If we consistently reinvest our dividends regardless of what we think the market might do next, then what we're doing is dollar cost averaging. Except on average, our dividend income will continually increase, because each time we reinvest, we increase the number of shares held. That's an important concept. With dividends we build streams of income. When markets go down, the dividend distribution is still based on the number of shares held. And we know that when markets are down, our reinvested dividends buy more shares than when markets are up. It's a building game that is somewhat disjointed from valuation. When we get to *Chapter 9: Benchmarking*, we'll see that we don't just want to benchmark the value of our portfolio; we also want to benchmark our quarterly dividend distributions. We want to see them progressively increase, and we want them to exceed predetermined values based on the amount of savings we plan to accumulate by each stage in our investment horizon.

In *Dividend Investing,* we discussed attributes to review before purchasing a stock, and we paid close attention to attributes that are particularly important to the dividend investor. We won't cover the same material here, but I do want to review a couple concepts that are particularly important to the dividend investor.

First, it never pays to chase after high dividends. Yes, the greater the yield, the greater the building blocks. But when a dividend gets too big, it's thought to be unstable, and when the dividend gets cut, the stock price will fall. So what we really want is a dividend that's reasonable and sustainable. The yield should be in line with those of other companies in the same sector. We also want a small payout ratio. That is, we want the distribution to be as small a percentage of the company's earnings per share as possible. A payout ratio around 30% is thought to be sustainable. For every dollar the company earns, they distribute $0.30 to their shareholders. But if the payout ratio gets up around 75% or higher, it's best to stay away. If earnings drop, the company could be forced to cut their dividend, and that's a loss that gets passed on to the shareholders.

Second, the S&P 500 Dividend Aristocrats is prime hunting ground for investments. We know that the constituents of this index have all increased their dividend every year for at least the past 25 years. That doesn't mean they pay huge dividends, it means they pay consistent and sustainable dividends. If you want a big dividend, this index will eventually provide it, but it's a waiting game. As these companies increase their dividends, it puts upward pressure on the stock price. This makes sense, because net income needs to increase in order for them to keep increasing their dividend for such a long stretch of time. So on average, we should see both the stock price and dividend distribution increase. As this happens, the yield could very well stay the same. Perhaps they increased their dividend by 2.5% because net income increased by 2.5%, and the market reacted with a similar increase to the stock price. It probably won't happen in exact proportions, but the idea is the same nonetheless. The dividend yield when measured as a percent of the stock's current selling price may be relatively stable. But the dividend yield when measured as a percent of your initial investment should increase with relative consistency. If, for example, you paid $15.37 per share 20 years ago and they keep increasing the dividend, then the current payout when measured as a percent of $15.37 will keep getting bigger and bigger.

We're playing the long game here, both with our dividends and with our capital gains. We're going to let markets work through their cycles. As we dollar cost average and periodically rebalance our portfolios, the markets do all the work; *they bring the gains to us*. And we'll use our dividend income to build more shares each and every step of the way.

What we want are steady and sustainable dividends that increase every year, even if it's gradual. *It doesn't get any more boring than that! And it's the closest thing to guaranteed success that we can find!*

**Our (*Mostly*) Boring Exit Point**

Entering the market with the exact same amount of money each month is a boring but safe approach. When it comes time to exit, we also desire an approach that is similarly boring but safe. At each stage in the investment horizon, there will be variables that are beyond our control. But come retirement, the variables are more profound because we no longer have time to see things through. Therefore, we need to do a thorough job of preparing for that which cannot be controlled.

If you're invested in a tax-deferred retirement account, then the exit point is more or less mandated. Starting at age 70 ½, you're required to make minimum annual withdrawals from your tax-deferred account. Even if just a portion of your investments are held in a tax-deferred account, you'll be required to make a withdrawal.

In *Chapter 1: Is $1 Million Enough?* we discussed the 4% rule. The initial intent of the rule is to spend 4% of your retirement savings in the first year, and then increase this amount by the rate of inflation in subsequent years. We also discussed an approach that's a bit more ambitious, and that's to structure the portfolio so that it yields at least 4% in dividend income. Given that we'll want to allocate greater than half the portfolio to bonds in the later years (*to protect our capital!*), our success with this goal is contingent on interest rates. During an economic crisis, the Feds can slash rates in an effort to accelerate growth. In other words, when markets flounder, the young get a great deal on their mortgage, and this is basically paid for by retirees who need the interest income to support themselves. When this happens, you might find yourself spending down a portion of the portfolio rather than surviving purely on the yield. And that's fine. The 4% rule, in its proposed form, isn't so much about yield as it is about spending the portfolio down gradually over 30 years. But that doesn't mean we won't strive to live off our distributions. When achievable, it's the safer alternative.

If you read *Dividend Investing,* then you might see where this is going. If 50% of your portfolio is allocated to bonds and the Feds slash interest rates, you're basically hosed. This will force you to eat into the capital that you planned to continue earning a return on for the rest of your life. In other words, low interest rates could dictate your exit point.

*Or will they?*

Long-term bond funds increase in value when interest rates head south (all because they have a higher interest rate locked in for an extended duration). So if you sell some shares of your long-term fund for a gain, you can reinvest the proceeds in higher-yielding equities, such as a REIT or preferred stock index. You might even want to buy some blue chips that have been beaten down. Some really good stock picks can be scavenged when interest rates are low. It's all about finding companies that don't cut their dividends during recessions, like the ones that constitute the S&P 500 Dividend Aristocrats.

Chances are good that these types of equities will be offering attractive yields when you need them. The economic conditions that force interest rates to get slashed are the same economic conditions that cause equities to be beaten down until the yield goes up. This, of course, assumes that markets behave similar to the way they've behaved in the past. Markets, as we know, are not static. Herd behavior will always create never before encountered situations. That's why we need to prepare for the unexpected.

*I know what you're thinking. We're breaking rules here.* We're moving in and out of asset classes based on yield instead of our rebalancing strategy. This is very different then letting the markets work through their cycles and bring the gains to us. *It's okay.* In retirement, it's not about building further wealth, it's about playing defense, and hanging on to a low-yielding asset class that has increased in value as interest rates are cut doesn't make sense. It also doesn't make sense to eat away at your capital when you could be earning something closer to the 4% yield that we're after. So make the change carefully. You don't have to sell all of your long-term bond holdings at once. In fact, you should only sell a portion of them. We still need safety. While dividend stocks provide stronger yields at certain times, they are not a replacement for bonds and do not provide the safety that bonds provide. So move gradually.

Start with a little. If conditions improve, resume with your rebalancing approach. If they get worse, sell some more long-term bonds and reinvest in stocks. Do it systematically and in tiny increments. We're not chasing excitement as we defend the portfolio. We don't want to move large portions of the portfolio in and out of different asset classes in an effort to chase the highest yield. Rather, we want to do so gradually and systematically. Even when conditions get rocky, we want the transition to be boring. We never want to completely abandon bonds just because interest rates are scraping the floor. We need safety. And there will be times when we must sacrifice strong yields in order to procure the safety we're after.

In retirement, there really are two kinds of exit points, those that you plan for and those that are forced upon you. The strategy just described is intended to add systematic order to a situation where the exit point has been forced.

Striving to maintain a 4% yield throughout retirement is a noble yet ambitious goal. There will be periods when it's achievable, and there will be periods when it isn't. A strong and sustainable stream of dividend income should provide a sense of safety. But more likely than not, you won't be able to just put the portfolio on cruise control. When things are good, it's time to prepare for an eventual, yet unpredictable, change in market direction.

If you achieve a dividend yield that is more than enough to live on, perhaps you'll want to take some shares off the table and keep a cash reserve so you don't find yourself selling into a bear market two or three years down the line. This would be another approach at exiting the market in an orderly and systematic manner. But you're doing it because the situation allows for it, not because you think you can call a market top. Picking tops and bottoms on your way to retirement is a dangerous game—*but doing so in retirement is even more dangerous*.

Many of us are going to sell investments along the way. If it's not because a golden opportunity is staring us in the eye, then maybe it's the need for liquidity. It can be scary when this need arrives during a bear market. If you've been contributing to a well-diversified portfolio for 20, 30, or even 40 years, a bear market will take a nice sized chunk out of your equities. That's why we want to both protect the portfolio with bonds as we hedge our losses with gold. But if you've been investing for this long, chances are good that you're still in the green.
A bear market is defined as a pullback of 20% or more from the market's most recent top. There's no limit on how far it can go, but the smart money is going to recognize a discount while it's on the table. Bottoms tend to form more quickly than tops. And when a long-term investor is forced to sell into a bear market, it generally means that they have to give back some gains. While giving back gains is never pleasant, it's much better than losing the cost of your initial investment.

Let's take a look from a historic perspective.

Going back to 1950, we see a number of periods where the market made significant pullbacks. It goes with the territory. But each and every time this happens, the market goes on to set new highs. A significant pullback that brings the market all the way back to the same lows as the last pullback is rare, but not unheard of.

If we hone in on just the 1960s and 1970s, we see that the market progressively made lower bottoms for the better part of a decade.

A retired investor who is forced to sell into one of these bottoms would have hopefully been heavily invested during the 1950s, and enjoyed a huge run-up prior to the pullback. Ideally, the investor would have progressively switched from stocks to bonds during the run-up, and would therefore have some protection during the repeated pullbacks. It should be noted that interest rates were significantly higher during these pullbacks than they are today, fluctuating between 4% and 13%.

During this period, a young investor would have a tremendous opportunity to implement a dollar cost averaging approach. The repeated dips would simultaneously pull down the average cost of investments while elevating the dividend yield. Of course, actual results from the era will not correspond exactly with the charts. Investors didn't have access to index funds, they had to pick individual stocks and bonds. While this approach would not be ideal in today's environment, a well-diversified portfolio that holds many stocks from all sectors would have performed relatively close to the market average.

The investor who adopted such an approach, remained invested over the long-haul, and was forced to sell into a market pullback would still come out ahead, though gains would be given back upon selling.

What about the investor who successfully maintains a yield on their portfolio of 4% or more? For this investor, there is no exit point. They will eventually bequeath the portfolio to a loved one. And if they did their estate planning right, the beneficiaries will receive a stepped up-basis in the assets. Say, for example, that the average cost paid for a fund is $100. If it is worth $130 at the time of bequeathment, the beneficiary will inherit their shares at a value of $130. If they later sell the shares at $140, they will only be taxed on the $10 gain that occurred after bequeathment.

In my opinion, this is the most boring way for an investor to exit the market. And that's exactly what we want. Later in life, preservation of capital is far more important than an opportunity to recognize gains. We want slow and steady returns, and we want there to be enough money to cover our needs . . . *and then some!* A good investment strategy is important, but the ability to execute and stay the course holds even greater importance.

At this stage in the game, we still strive for boredom. But when the market dictates "excitement," we strive to react in the most boring manner possible.

# Chapter 5

## Asset Allocation

Asset allocation is the cornerstone of a successful investment strategy. And just like our entry and exit points, *we want it to be (mostly) boring!*

At this point, we've accrued some savings and will continually fund the portfolio. And we're going to rely on dollar cost averaging to systematically acquire shares at below average prices. Next, we need to ensure that we're picking the right investments.

What constitutes the "right" investment will change over time. That's because early on, we want investments that are going to grow. We want big capital gains (with a bit of dividend income on the side). A healthy portion of the portfolio should be allocated to equities that are expected to increase substantially over time. We want them to increase by more than the rate of inflation. As we get older and the portfolio gets bigger, the approach changes, albeit gradually. We now have something worth protecting. And we're progressively getting closer to the point where we'll want to implement the 4% rule. In order to survive on distributions and not have to liquidate our holdings, we need strong and sustainable dividends.

*Dividend Investing* provides a thorough breakdown of stocks, bonds, and real estate. It explores different sectors and the benefits of adding foreign markets to the portfolio. For purposes of *Preparing For Financial Success,* we're going to assume an effective yet simpler approach to asset allocation.

We'll be investing in the same asset classes, while focusing our attention exclusively on index funds that provide broad exposure to domestic markets. Although opportunities for further diversification are available, they're not paramount to success.

With additional sophistication comes additional complexity. My recommendation is to start with simple yet adequate tools. Obtain a firm understanding of the investment strategy and begin the process of building your portfolio. With time, the structure of the portfolio can be modified, and opportunities to add further diversification, if desired, can be coupled with further reading and a deeper understanding of the different market sectors. The books reviewed in *Chapter 10: Further Reading* are an excellent place to start.

Come retirement, dividend yield is import. While we won't reiterate the benefit of different market sectors and geographical regions that's covered in *Dividend Investing*, we will review some ways to increase yield through moderate exposure to riskier asset classes. We're also going to talk about gold.

Given that gold doesn't pay a dividend, it wasn't covered in *Dividend Investing*, but it's still a valuable hedge that can provide tremendous benefit to the portfolio. Like anything else, the key is to allocate the appropriate percentage of the portfolio to this commodity. We'll get to this shortly. But first, let's review our dividend payers with regard to how they'll be used to structure your portfolio.

## Stocks

We're going to start with stocks simply because the stock market is the most recognized investment market in the world. When someone says they're invested in "the market," stocks immediately come to mind. While many markets exist, an exorbitant proportion of retirement savings is invested in the stock market. From a risk-reward standpoint, this is one of the riskier asset classes, yet the stock market has a history of always bouncing back from its lows. And it has a history of always beating inflation over extended periods of time, with the average return for the S&P 500 being 10% annually when invested in for 10 years or longer.

When we purchase stock, what we're really buying is an ownership interest. For better or worse, we are now owners of the company. And with that ownership interest comes the right to vote . . . *and that's about it.* From a theoretical standpoint, I've never quite understood the value of this right, at least as far as the little guy is concerned. And that's what most retirement investors are—*we're the little guys.*

My right to vote is as small as my investment. It doesn't hold the same weight as when the CEO of Berkshire Hathaway casts his vote (because he has a lot more shares). When I purchase and sell stocks, it doesn't move markets like it does for Warren Buffett. So when I invest in a company, I'm not really buying an ownership interest in the sense that it comes with any sort of meaningful vote. Instead, I'm buying the right to fly on the coattails of Warren Buffet, Carl Icahn, George Soros, and other influential investors. When I buy an index fund like the SPDR S&P 500 ETF (SPY), I gain an ownership interest in 500 different stocks. But again, I don't have any voting rights. I can't have a meaningful impact on the underlying businesses. I'm merely along for the ride. And that's fine, because there's safety in numbers.

Depending on the type of stocks invested in, we can weight the portfolio in favor of large capital gains, we can weight the portfolio in favor of dividend income, or we can use broad market exposure to obtain a combination of the two.

For the new investor, holding a fund that tracks the S&P 500 is sufficient. It provides exposure to all 11 market sectors. While this alone won't make the portfolio diversified, it's a huge step in the right direction. And this exposure can be obtained at very little cost. At time of writing, the SPY only charges an annual expense ratio of 0.09%.

**Bonds**

Bonds provide safety. These are predictable investments. When we purchase a bond, it comes with a stated interest payment. Should we hold the bond to maturity, we earn the interest and receive our principal back. It's a safe and boring way to earn a return while protecting a portion of the portfolio from the periodic downturns we expect to encounter with our equity investments.

This doesn't mean that the value of a bond fund doesn't fluctuate. If you decide to sell a bond before it matures, the amount that you'll be able to sell it for is contingent on the current interest rate. We discussed this above as we searched for a boring exit point during times when interest rates are slashed. What we saw is that the price of a bond is inversely related to a change in the interest rate. When interest rates are cut, the value of an existing bond goes up. And when interest rates go up, the value of an existing bond goes down.

This makes sense, because what a bond does is it locks in a rate. If you've locked yourself in at 3% and the going interest rate is increased to 3.5%, then your bond should decline in value. Higher yielding bonds are now available, and this means that rational investors are no longer willing to pay full price for the bond you hold. The longer you're locked in at 3%, the larger the decline. This might sound discouraging, but you can think of the glass as being half-full rather than half-empty. When interest rates are cut, the value of an existing bond increases. The longer you're locked in at the higher interest rate, the larger the increase.

When we buy a bond fund, we acquire many bonds in one shot. The fund might represent the entire bond market or the fund might be geared towards a specific type of bond, say short-term Treasuries, or maybe long-term corporate bonds. Depending on the type of bonds held, the fund will fluctuate in accordance to the economic environment.

Even though we buy bond funds for safety, they still exhibit some volatility, but they do so to a much smaller degree than our equity holdings. The safety we gain from bond funds is very real, even though they fluctuate. It's important to understand that not all bonds are created equal and not all bonds provide the same degree of safety. Like any other investment, as we move from the safest bond issues to the riskiest bond issues, our expected return should increase. Otherwise, only the safest bonds would sell. When riskier bonds are purchased in large quantities by means of a fund, there's still a sense of safety in that a single issue going into default won't drag down the entire fund. We're not concerned with the impact of a single security, though we are still concerned with the impact that economic events can have on the greater bond market.

For our purpose, a bond fund that holds Treasuries with varying maturities is sufficient. The iShares U.S. Treasury Bond ETF (GOVT) is a popular fund with a low expense ratio, currently charging 0.15%. The dividend yield currently rests at 1.96%. For many, a Treasury fund is the centerpiece of their bond holdings. But the investor who's comfortable accepting additional risk, along with additional return, might want to invest in the Vanguard Total Bond Market Index Fund ETF (BND). This fund, which aims to represent the entire domestic bond market, including both Treasuries and corporate bonds, currently yields 2.73% and has an exceptionally low expense ratio of 0.03%. The investor who is comfortable accepting additional risk from here, perhaps in an effort to achieve an overall 4% yield on their retirement savings, can branch off into even riskier funds. Bond funds with long durations will typically yield more than funds with short durations. Corporate bonds typically offer higher yields than Treasuries, given that the bonds aren't backed by the taxing authority of the U.S. Government. The risk adverse investor might even allocate a small portion of the portfolio to junk bonds; they offer much higher yields than investment grade corporate bonds. And if the subprime mortgage crisis of 2008 didn't frighten you too badly, a mortgage REIT can be added to further increase the overall yield on your portfolio.

Should you decide to branch off into higher yielding funds, my advice is to use either a Treasury fund, such as GOVT, or a total market fund, such as BND, as the nucleus of your bond holdings. These types of funds provide adequate diversification within the bond market. Higher-yielding funds can then be added in appropriate increments in order to increase overall yield on the portfolio. A hefty allocation that favors investment grade corporate bonds is prudent for the risk averse investor. Funds that hold riskier issues, such as junk bonds and mortgage REITs, should be added in smaller increments, if desired.

Adding a junk bond fund that yields 6% will drive up the overall yield on the portfolio, but it will also increase risk. The great thing about high yielders is that a small allocation makes a difference. If Treasuries are only yielding 2%, then every dollar of the portfolio that's added to junk bonds will earn three times the return of every dollar that's invested in Treasuries. So it's possible to get the punch that you're after with just a small allocation.

Say you have $10,000 allocated to bonds. If allocated entirely to Treasuries, your annual return will be $200.

10,000 x 2% = $200

However, if 10% of the bond holdings are reallocated to junk bonds, the yield increases by 20%.

9,000 x 2% = 180

1,000 x 6% = 60

180 + 60 = 240

(240 – 200) / 200 = 20%

By combining different bond funds in appropriate proportions, the increase to your return exceeds the increase in the level of risk.

It's important to note that the junk bond allocation is 10% of the bond allocation, not 10% of the greater portfolio. Junk bonds are risky investments that should only comprise a small percentage of the portfolio, say somewhere around 5%. If other risky investments are added in order to increase yield, it should be done in small increments. There's an even greater advantage if the risky holdings don't exhibit high levels of positive correlation—*in other words, we don't want them all to behave the same way when we experience changes in the economic environment.*

As stated before, the Vanguard Total Bond Market Index Fund ETF (BND) is sufficient for our purposes, especially for new investors. It provides the safety we're after and also provides diversification within the bond market. The yield, of course, is contingent on the rate set by the Federal Open Market Committee and will vary significantly over the course of your investment horizon.

**Real Estate**

As with stocks and bonds, we can gain broad exposure to the real estate market by means of a single fund. The Vanguard Real Estate Index Fund ETF (VNQ) provides broad exposure to the domestic real estate market, and like the funds mentioned above, does so for an extremely low fee. At the time of writing, it charges 0.12%.

This fund doesn't hold any real estate directly. Rather, it holds an index of REITs, and each of these REITs has a direct ownership in the real estate that they manage. This might sound like a derivative, but it's not. Instead, it's a two-tiered approach. By investing in the fund, you secure an ownership interest in a large number of REITs, all of which have various ownership interests in real estate.

This is a simple way to gain broad exposure to the real estate market. Where a bond investor might decide to forgo the fund approach and purchase bonds directly, it would be difficult to do the same with real estate. There's a boatload of paperwork, insurance, taxes, tenant agreements, *and so much more*, involved with making a direct investment in real estate. It's a lot of work and definitely not the way I plan to spend my weekends. But some people like it. In fact, you can make a lot of money with rental properties if you know what you're doing. But to gain broad diversification within the real estate market, investing in REITs is essential, and buying an index fund that represents the broader market makes things even easier.

Just like stocks, real estate is an equity interest. When we buy it, we gain an ownership interest, and we expect two results from our investment: (1) on average, we expect our investment to appreciate in value over the long-haul, and (2) we expect to receive distributions along the way.

When it comes to dividends, REITs provide an added sense of stability. In order for a real estate company to qualify as a REIT, they are required to distribute at least 90% of their rental income to investors in the form of a dividend. This is the type of boredom that we're after. Where a publicly traded company is at liberty to reduce or eliminate their stock dividend and the Feds are at liberty to slash interest rates, REITs are required to distribute 90% of their rental income. The income is steady and, under most market conditions, predictable. And that's important to consider when determining the weight of each asset class in your portfolio.

REITs provide a sense of safety in that a distribution will be made, but don't forget that it's still an equity holding. They don't keep your invested capital safe the way bonds do. Just like stocks, they can be subject to a market crash, and some of these crashes can be deep. The financial crisis of 2008 is an obvious example.

It can devastate a portfolio when two separate equity markets are hit simultaneously, and that's exactly what happened during the financial crisis. Both stocks and real estate headed south in unison. There's no guarantee that this won't happen again. But a benefit to investing in multiple equity markets is that they aren't always subjected to pullbacks at the same time. We'll discuss correlation in more detail when we get to *Chapter 7: Rebalancing*, and then dive into the theory behind it in *Chapter 8: Why it Works*. But as I've stated before, and will continue to state throughout the book, the process of rebalancing doesn't just help maintain our desired level of risk, it forces us to buy low and sell high.

There will be times when the real estate market moves in conjunction with the stock market, but the true benefit of investing in both markets can be seen when the markets diverge. If real estate goes up while stocks trend down, then we recognize some gains on our real estate in order to reinvest in the stock market while it's priced at a discount. If real estate trends down as stocks advance, then we do just the opposite. And when all of our equity holdings trend down at the same time, we see the true benefit in maintaining our allocation in both bonds and gold.

Broad exposure to the real estate market is extremely beneficial. Its short-term movements won't always align with those of the stock market. This increases the safety of the portfolio while creating a rebalancing opportunity. Over the long haul, our REIT holdings are expected to provide capital gains combined with a strong dividend yield. It's a healthy mix of growth and dividends, and it increase the diversification of the portfolio.

**Diversification**

Note that for each ETF discussed above, I stated that they provide adequate diversification "*within*" the market. This is an important distinction, because owning the entire stock market does not make your portfolio diversified. Neither does owning the entire bond market, nor the entire real estate market. In fact, if you look at the prospectus for each of the funds mentioned above, you'll see that each fund is advertised as being non-diversified. That's because simply being diversified within a market doesn't count as diversification. If all you hold is the entire stock market and the stock market tanks, your portfolio will suffer. The same applies if all you hold is the entire bond market or the entire real estate market. And if all you hold is gold, then you've got a rough ride ahead.

It's not enough to be diversified within a market. It might protect you in the event that a specific stock sector takes a hit or an isolated region of your real estate holdings falls victim to a natural disaster, but it doesn't protect you when the entire stock market crashes and it won't keep you safe from the next financial crisis. So we're going to invest in all three markets discussed above, and also keep some gold in the portfolio as an additional hedge.

**Gold**

Gold is a hedge and nothing more. In my opinion, it should constitute no more than 10% of the portfolio. For starters, it's not boring. There might be times when it seems like it's boring, but that's just because gold is good at playing possum. When other investments perform poorly, gold has a habit of sneaking up with some excitement. In fact, gold is a bit rebellious. It's known to do the exact opposite of equities. It won't stand in line. It doesn't follow the herd. It refuses to pay a dividend. And when everything else tanks, there's a fairly good probability that it's going to shoot through the roof.

In conservative increments, it's okay to place boring on the back burner and add some excitement to the portfolio. It will pay off over the long-run if you don't have too much riding on it.

In college, I had a finance professor teach us that when you buy gold, you want it to decline in value. If it does, it means your other investments are probably doing just fine. But when that's not the case, you'll be glad you have some gold in the portfolio. When the stock market crashes, the herd claims that wealth has been lost. But we know that that's simply not true. Wealth isn't lost during a crash, it's merely transferred, and those who hold gold are the victors. It's difficult to predict when exactly gold is going to make its move. Sometimes it moves gradually, sometimes it provides a quick burst to the upside, and sometimes it loses money while the rest of your holdings prosper. This is the nature of a hedge, and it's important to keep your exposure conservative.

Remember, the average bull market lasts 4.5 years and the average bear market lasts 14 months. Therefore, gold should be a small part of the portfolio, because the spans during which gold outperforms will be shorter than the spans during which equities outperform. Based on these figures, you can expect to be in a bull market 80% of the time, and in a bear market for the other 20%. So it makes sense not to allocate more than 10% of the portfolio to gold (and maybe even less). Remember, bonds also provide protection during a bear market. Real estate may or may not follow suit with stocks. It's a crap shoot. The investor who starts in her 20s and continues to invest up into her 60s will encounter situations where stocks and real estate move in unison, and then encounter other situations where they don't. But when equity markets decline simultaneously, you'll be happy to have some gold in the portfolio.

I hate to keep harping on the 2008 financial crisis, but it's an excellent example. When stocks and real estate tanked, gold shot through the roof. It took almost ten years for stocks to pass gold again, and real estate is still catching up. For those who stayed the course and implemented a rebalancing strategy, they'd have systematically sold off shares of their gold fund while picking up stocks and real estate at huge discounts. Ten years later, they'd finally be selling some of their stock fund to buy more gold, and doing so will put them in a great position for the next crash.

It's interesting to note that gold didn't really take off until 2010. It actually starts to go down at the beginning of the crisis, just like stocks and real estate. This is one of those rare situations where *everyone* panicked and *everything* went down . . . at least at first. Gold turns course roughly six months in advance of equities and then there's no catching it. As I said, gold doesn't stand in line and it doesn't follow the herd. Its rebellion should be noted. Though unpredictable, it has a history of getting the job done.

Most market timers don't have the patience to wait two full years after a crash for gold to make its move. At that point, recovery wasn't far away, and equities would soon begin a slow but steady advance that would eventually bring markets to new heights. If in 2010 you bought equities instead of gold and then just let it ride, you'd have done well. But if just a tiny portion of the portfolio were allocated to gold, you'd have done so much better. It initially appeared that gold wasn't going to work its magic—*but it did.* We all know that markets can remain irrational longer than most investors can remain solvent. That's why we shy away from market timing. An investor who allocates 10% of the portfolio towards gold, rebalances periodically, and sees things through would walk away from the crash and subsequent recovery better than an investor who only invests in stocks, bonds, and real estate.

It's times like these that the 10% allocated to gold packs its punch. It's difficult to predict exactly when the punch is coming—*two years later?*—but gold has a tendency to eventually come through with a knockout blow. The asset allocator doesn't have to predict when it's coming, she simply needs to stay the course and recognize some gains on her gold fund through the process of rebalancing.

The truth is, we like gold for the same reason we like companies that consistently increase their dividend each year. In other words, we like gold because it can't be manipulated. A country can enact fiscal policy to manipulate its currency, and there's nothing to stop them from printing unhealthy volumes of their currency. This type of manipulation gives rise to inflation. Gold serves as a valuable hedge against inflation purely because it can't be manipulated. There's a limited quantity in the world, and its value is a product of demand.

For each of the markets discussed above, I provided an example of a popular fund that can be used to gain broad market exposure. These aren't endorsements of specific products, but rather a means of highlighting funds that investors commonly use when applying this approach. I'm not going to do the same for gold, mainly because the best method of investing in gold is open for debate.

True gold connoisseurs will tell you that taking physical possession of gold is the only way to go. And there've been allegations that some gold ETFs don't actually hold as much gold as they imply, but instead invest at least a portion of their capital in derivatives designed to track the price of gold.

There's always a risk involved when you don't physically take possession of your investment. Sometimes the risk is unavoidable. With real estate, it's impossible for the average investor to gain adequate diversification by taking physical possession of property. The ETF solves this problem. But with gold, it's actually quite easy to possess the commodity. The ETF doesn't reduce risk, but rather, increases the risk that you're invested in derivatives rather than the actual commodity. Additionally, storing gold properly costs money. Like anything else, fees are involved. Even if you invest in an ETF, the ETF must pay to store the gold in their possession, and this fee is indirectly passed along to the investor.

As we dive deeper into our rebalancing strategy, you'll see that there's a benefit to holding gold in an ETF that trades on an open exchange. It's really easy to buy and sell shares as you realign your portfolio with your desired level of risk. I'm not going to propagate ETFs as the safest way to invest in gold, but they do provide a level of convenience that's difficult to resist.

## Asset Allocation

Now that we have a better understanding of the markets we'll be investing in, let's define asset allocation and take a closer look at its workings. According to Investopedia, asset allocation is an investment strategy that aims to balance risk and reward by apportioning a portfolio's assets according to an individual's goals, risk tolerance, and investment horizon.

We know that equities are risky, and we should expect higher average returns for assuming this risk. In the early years, we'll want to overweight the portfolio in favor of these investments and underweight the bond allocation. As we age, we become more vulnerable to market pullbacks. A bear market is actually our friend early on because it provides an opportunity to acquire investments while markets are priced below their moving average—*and they often remain below their average for extended periods of time!* A crash can be devastating, but if we continue to make investments each month, we'll get some great discounts that will provide strong yields for the rest of our lives. The unfortunate part of this is that we all reach a point where we don't have ample time to recover from a crash. I wish it weren't the case, but it is. Watching your portfolio get cut in half when your highest earning years are in the past is traumatizing. The advice traditionally given by investment advisors is to gradually shift from equities to bonds as you age. A common rule of thumb is to own your age in bonds. If you're 45 years old, you would allocate 45% of your portfolio to bonds and the remaining 55% would be allocated amongst stocks, real estate, and perhaps some exposure to gold. I like to assume a bit more risk with the intent of earning a higher reward throughout my investing career. For this reason, I like to allocate my age minus 10 years to bonds, with the rest allocated to stocks, bonds, and just a touch of gold. It's a riskier position than many investors assume, but I'm comfortable with the risk.

Some investors like to maintain a cash reserve. It allows them to buy up assets when they become unusually cheap. If you decide to keep idle cash in the portfolio, don't consider it part of the bond allocation. Yes, cash is almost as safe as bonds. There is, of course, an inflation rate risk that you assume by only earning the money market rate (rather than at least earning the three-month Treasury rate). But the true purpose in holding idle cash is to buy up stocks and REITs when either the market or a specific security becomes extremely underpriced. For this reason, it's best to treat idle cash as part of your allocation to equities. And remember, it's dangerous to wait for a lucrative entry point, because the best entry point that you'll ever see again may very well pass you by. So if you do hold idle cash, keep it small, nothing larger than 5%.

While a cash holding can be viewed as safe, it's the split between equities and bonds the truly defines our tolerance for risk. By "tolerance for risk," I'm referring to one's willingness to take on riskier investments in an effort to achieve higher returns. It's different for everyone, and much of the tolerance pertains to one's capacity to see things through during a recession. Generally speaking, the higher the risk, the greater the reward. But there's a huge difference between taking on so much risk that you guarantee your own failure and upping the level of risk to something appropriate for your personality, age, and financial situation. If you're going to get scared and sell your assets after they've dropped in value, then you need to allocate the majority of your portfolio into risk free Treasury notes or bonds and only assume minor exposure to equities. Your returns won't be impressive, but you'll never have to watch your portfolio cycle through a downturn.

If you're the type of person who doesn't even bother logging into your brokerage account during a recession because you have confidence that the market will bounce back, then you should weight the portfolio more heavily towards equities as you minimize your exposure to Treasuries. There are literally hundreds of variations between these two extremes. That's part of what makes investing fun. It's also part of the reason why herd mentality doesn't completely cannibalize the investment world. We all have differing tolerances for risk, and this provides a healthy dose of sobriety to the recklessness of herd mentality.

We keep lumping stocks and real estate together when it comes to risk, but it's important to note that our equity holdings won't necessarily behave the same way throughout the glut of economic environments that we're going to face. The fact that real estate tends to beat stocks during periods of inflation but does worse than stocks during periods of disinflation, means that the two asset classes will serve as good compliments within the portfolio.

Growth is important early on, but the closer we get to retirement, the more stable we want the portfolio to be. And while it's impossible to always earn large capital gains, by controlling for risk, we can strive to earn modest yet steady capital gains as we collect our dividends. While risk tolerance is indeed different for every investor, our common goal is to build wealth from which we will earn a stream of dividend income for the rest of our lives. The capital dedicated to this endeavor should be significant, and over time, we should make changes to our risk tolerance to ensure that our accumulated wealth is safe.

## Correlation

So far we've discussed what asset allocation is. We've gone over the types of markets we want to invest in. We know that we'll need to determine our tolerance for risk in order to allocate the right amount of money to each of these markets. We understand to some extent that we don't always want our investments to move in the same direction at the same time. And whatever happens, we don't ever want to get scared and sell in the middle of a bear market (as this will completely destroy the portfolio).

But how exactly do we determine our asset allocation? What's this rebalancing thing all about? Will it really force us to buy low and sell high without having to predict market direction? And if so, how does it all work? The simplest answer is that it all comes down to correlation. Do the assets we've invested in move in the same or different directions under various economic conditions?

Essentially, we want to invest in different assets that do not exhibit a high degree of positive correlation. Positive correlation is when different assets move in the same direction at the same time. They don't necessarily need to be moving at the same pace, just in the same direction. One asset can be going up faster than another, but if they are both moving in an upward trend, then they are said to be positively correlated. The same terminology applies when different assets trend downward at the same time. The more time they spend moving in the same direction, the stronger the correlation. If they have a history of only moving in the same direction during very specific, or even random, intervals, then the correlation is said to be weak, though it's still positive if the times during which they behave the same exceed the times during which they don't. It's also worth noting that correlation is not static. Two assets can exhibit a high degree of positive correlation for an extended period of time, but this can change, and market factors may force them to stop exhibiting any correlation at all.

By diversifying our portfolio into funds that do not exhibit strong positive correlation, we not only minimize the size of a potential decline in portfolio value, but also minimize the duration of time during which the portfolio stays in the red. This provides safety against both mild and severe pullbacks.

If we were to invest in 100 different REITs and nothing more, the portfolio would not be considered diversified just because 100 is a large number. There are market conditions that will affect all real estate investments in either a positive or negative manner. There are also conditions that will affect some REITs but not others.

Some properties are going to be better managed than others. Some geographical regions are more susceptible to natural disaster. And commercial real estate is currently doing battle with ecommerce, while residential real estate faces different obstacles. Different circumstances will affect different properties, but this doesn't change the fact that certain economic events, such as a change in interest rates or the tax code, can affect all REITs simultaneously. Because of this, most of the 100 holdings are going to exhibit strong positive correlation, which means that to seek safety, we must diversify into other markets.

The overarching goal is to minimize the impact of market downturns by holding other markets that simultaneously prosper. If most of our holdings pay a distribution of some sort, be it a dividend, rent, or interest payment, then the portfolio will increase in value as losses are averaged out against gains. If we implement a rebalancing strategy, then we're not just talking about losses being averaged out against gains. We're talking about gains being recognized while our losing assets serve as discount material for further investment. The benefit of rebalancing is strong. When we combine this approach with a variety of markets that will beat inflation over the long-haul, the impact multiplies. It's just like the benefit of compounding our dividends over an extended period of time, and there's no reason why we can't implement both of these strategies simultaneously.

If market correlation is a new concept, then it might feel very theoretical at this point, and the applicability may not yet be obvious. We'll dissect the theory further in *Chapter 8: Why it Works*. But for now, let's have a closer look at the role dividends play in building our portfolio.

# Chapter 6

## Dividend Income and The Power of Compounding

From a compounding perspective, dividends play an important role throughout the entire investment horizon. We use them to build. The power of earning dividend income on top of reinvested dividend income on top of even more reinvested dividend income cannot be overemphasized. It's a powerful building tool that should be utilized at every stage of the investment horizon.

Most investors are concerned with the total value of the portfolio, as they should be. Bet when it comes to measuring success, this is just one of several important measures. There are many intricate pieces used to form a well-balanced portfolio, and so long as the portfolio is kept safe, how much it yields is equally as important as how much it's worth. The dividend investor doesn't just count dollars, she counts income, which means she also counts shares. This is a metric that most investors don't put much weight into, but it's really important. *Why?* Because dividends are paid on a per share basis. Every month we receive dividends, and every month we should reinvest those dividends. Even when markets go up, we can increase the number of holdings through reinvestment, which in turn increases our dividend income. And when markets go down, we can increase the number of holdings by even more, which in turn increases our dividend income by even more. This is important because market pullbacks are temporary, but the increased dividend income is perpetual. For however long we hold the security, we expect to receive distributions.

Like all investors, the dividend investor will face setbacks, and she can take precautions to hedge against those setbacks. The most profound setback a dividend investor can incur is when the Feds slash interest rates after she reaches retirement. I won't reiterate the strategy discussed above—*if you need a reminder, you'll want to gradually sell your long-term bond funds at a gain as you reinvest in higher-yielding markets*—but instead want to focus on ways to increase dividend yield in retirement.

It's tempting to overweight in favor of high yielding investments. But remember, the higher the yield, the higher the risk. This doesn't mean that there isn't room in the portfolio for a junk bond fund, or even a mortgage REIT fund. It simply means that we want to proceed cautiously and maintain a high degree of safety as we add higher yielding investments to the portfolio in conservative increments.

To fully understand the benefits of safely increasing your dividend yield, think about what an extra half percent means. If you're yielding 3% on your portfolio and can find a way to safely increase the yield by 0.5%, then your income will increase by 16.67% (0.005 / 0.03 = 0.1667). That's not too shabby an increase to your income. It's significantly more than the annual pay increase most of us expect to receive from our employer. But it's also easier said than done.

*So how do we go about increasing our dividend income while keeping the portfolio safe?*

The overarching goal is to achieve a 4% yield on the portfolio. This allows us to follow the 4% rule without ever eating into our principal. We have to acknowledge that it will be easy at certain points and difficult at others. It all comes down to the going interest rate. Let's discuss this from a historic perspective, and then take a look at some high yielding securities that can be used in small increments to add an additional punch to our dividend income.

**Bonds**

Bonds by and large are the biggest variable when it comes to the yield you can expect from your portfolio. In retirement we want safety, which means we want lots and lots of Treasury bonds. But we also want income, which means we need a decent yield from our bonds—*hopefully 4%.*

If we go back to 1990 and analyze the historic rate of Treasuries, we see that the average yield of the 3-month Treasury is only 2.79%. But this doesn't mean that an investor should anticipate returns of 2.79% in retirement. The 3-month Treasury is often used as a gauge for inflation. It's the safest bond you can buy, and therefore, the interest paid will keep pace with inflation and nothing more. If you want more interest then you have to assume more risk, and we'll discuss ways to do that. But first, let's have a closer look at historic yields on 3-month Treasuries.

Back in the 1980s, inflation was extremely high. Investors were earning close to 8% on risk-free Treasuries. It's a great yield, but it also means that the spending power of their principal was declining. For the investor who managed to build a $1,000,000 portfolio, an 8% yield would be the equivalent of an $80,000 annual salary. Keep in mind, $1,000,000 was a lot more in 1990 than it is today. Even with abnormally high inflation, an investor didn't need $1,000,000 to live comfortably.

As we progress into the onset of the 1990s, the 3-month Treasury yield gradually increased to a high of 8.26% and then started a gradual (albeit healthy) decline. By late 1991, it was down to 5%. An investor that only held 3-month Treasuries would have seen their income slashed by 40% (0.0825 – 0.05 / 0.0825 = 0.40), although they would still exceed the 4% that we're after. By the end of 1992 that wouldn't be the case, as rates dropped down below 3%.

That's the thing about interest. The rates change. Sometimes for the better, sometimes for the worse. It was 1994 before rates bounced back above 4%. They remained strong throughout the remainder of the 1990s, building up to nearly 6% by the time the dotcom bubble burst. In the years that followed, rates fell below 2%. That's the common market cycle we experience when it comes to interest rates. The Feds slash them in an effort to restore economic stability. It's the retirees who suffer as the younger population enjoys low mortgage rates and the opportunity to buy a new car at a reasonable price in spite of carrying a poor credit score.

It's important to note that this is not a natural market cycle. It's controlled by the Federal Open Market Committee, which includes members of the Federal Reserve. While this market cycle is steered by an authoritative body, it forces long-term bonds to exhibit weak correlation when compared to equities. The Feds are cutting rates because equities are suffering. But if you own a long-term bond fund that has higher rates locked in, you can expect the value of that fund to increase. The higher interest payments will persist until the underlying bonds mature and the fund replaces them with newer, lower-yielding issues. But that's okay. It gives the retired investor an opportunity to react. And hopefully they did, because in mid-2003 yields dipped below 1% and stayed that way for the better part of a year. Then, as should be expected, they began a gradual increase, returning to *normal* levels before the 2008 financial crisis.

In 2007, rates were above 5%. By late 2008, rates were close to zero. The subprime mortgage crisis was the largest financial crisis of our lifetime (*thus far*). Interest rates were almost non-existent. That means a retiree who has half of his portfolio allocated to bonds basically watched half of his income disappear. Most were forced to eat into principal, an act that reduces the number of shares they hold, resulting in smaller dividend payments for the rest of their lives.

By 2019, rates have only risen as high as 2.35%, and the Federal Open Market Committee is indicating that they'll cut rates rather than increase them. It's a preemptive strike of sorts, as the economy is performing well and employment is under control. But they're cutting rates nonetheless, and for retirees, it means they need to take a portion of their 4% out of principal rather than interest.

What we've seen here is a 30 year roller coaster ride. Interest rates were sky-high at the onset of the 1990s and proceeded to ebb and flow as equity markets became overpriced and crashed, only to become overpriced and then crash again. Just look at the chart below. It's astounding what the herd can do to itself. Sometimes the lessons learned are never repeated, other times we see the herd make the same foolish mistakes over and over again. And while the results can be cyclical, it's difficult to predict when exactly the herd has had enough and is ready to succumb to the cycle.

To put the weight of changing interest rates in perspective, let's measure the change in the 3-month T-bill rate against the appreciation of the Dow Jones Industrial average over the 10-year period following the financial crisis.

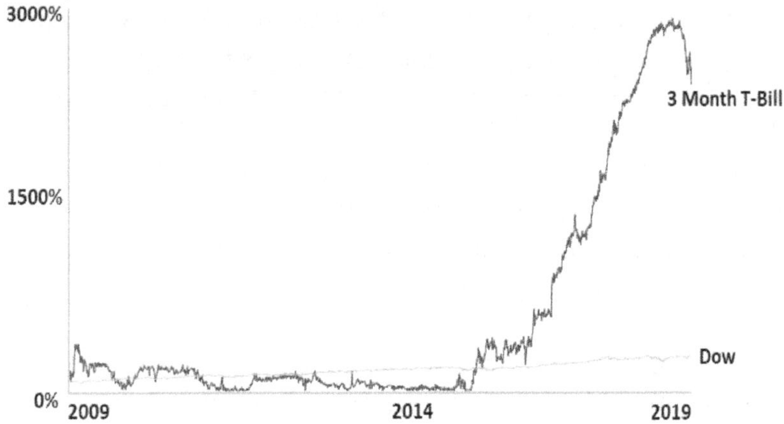


Note the interest paid on the 3-month T-bill appreciates be nearly 3000%. It seems astonishing, doesn't it? But remember, this doesn't equate to a 3000% return. Rather, it's a 3000% increase in your distribution. The interest rate was close to zero at the start of the period (0.08% to be precise). So increasing it to something that's, *well . . . at least noticeable*, will equate to a 3000% increase. The Dow Jones Industrial Average, on the other hand, appreciated by 188%. Of course, it's not an apples-to-apples comparison. We're comparing an increase in interest rates against capital appreciation. But there's still a takeaway, and the takeaway says something about volatility. What it says is that the

Federal Open Market Committee has the authority to make or break the yield on a retiree's portfolio, all depending on where they set the interest rate. It could be close to zero. Or it could be 3000% higher . . . *and then some!* This power makes the size of our returns extremely volatile, and much more than the volatility we expect from an equity holding.

Throughout retirement—an era in our lives that could conceivably last greater than 30 years—the repeated rise and fall of interest rates will have a profound impact on our income. But even during the down times, it's not the end of the world. The 4% rule was intended to deplete principal over the course of retirement. Yes, we're trying to do better than that. To some extent, we can do better. And to some extent, our success is contingent on where the Federal Open Market Committee decides to set interest rates.

While a Treasury fund should serve as the nucleus of your bond allocation, it doesn't constitute the entire portfolio. Let's have a look at other securities that can be used to increase your portfolio yield.

**Corporate bonds**

A great way to increase yield with only a small increase to risk is to diversify into corporate bonds. A corporation is forced to pay what is known as a risk premium. Treasuries don't offer a risk premium because they are backed by the taxing authority of the U.S. Government. Corporations have no taxing authority, so there's a chance that they might default on their bonds.

Just because corporate bonds offer a risk premium doesn't mean there aren't any similarities between corporate issues and Treasuries. Both Treasuries and corporate bonds have interest rate risk. That's why I recommend investing in a long-term bond fund. You can do better than the 3-month Treasury rate with longer-term Treasuries, say up to 20 years or more. The same applies to corporate bonds. The longer the duration, the higher the interest rate premium.

The risk involved is that interest rates will increase after you've locked in your rate, so you should expect to receive a premium for assuming this risk on a long-term investment. At the same time, if they cut rates, you're in the clear. You should expect the resale value of your holding to increase.

An additional risk that comes with corporate bonds is call risk. A call provision allows the issuer to repurchase and retire the bond. The issuer will exercise the call provision when interest rates are cut, as this prevents them from making payments that exceed the now lower market rate. This type of provision is designed to benefit the issuer at the expense of the investor. Should interest rates go up, the issuer will be content to keep making payments at the lower rate. The bondholder is left in a situation that is essentially lose-lose. When rates are cut, the issuer can call the bond, and the investor's next best option is to reinvest the funds in a newer issue with a smaller payment. As a result, investors are paid a premium for accepting a call provision, and this will increase their yield until the bond is called.

The potential to earn more with corporate bonds is obvious. The investor will receive premiums for accepting both the default risk and the call risk (if applicable). And just like

Treasuries, there is also interest rate risk. In fact, a long duration doesn't just increase the interest rate risk, but also increases the period of time over which a bond can be called or go into default. The premiums will vary according to the issue, and the company's financial position will have a direct impact on the premium paid for the applicable risk factors.

A host of variables impact the size of the premium, with the culmination of these variables influencing a rating that the bond receives from one of three agencies: Standard & Poor's, Moody's, and Fitch Group. The credit rating agencies have tremendous influence over the price of a bond. A bond rating of AAA to BBB- is considered investment grade, where a rating of BB+ to D is considered non-investment grade.

Yes, corporate bonds are riskier than Treasuries. But we can mitigate the risk of a specific issue by investing in a fund that holds many investment grade corporate bonds. By doing so, we reduce our risk to factors that affect the entire bond market, rather than being exposed to factors that affect a specific issue.

At the time of writing, the iShares iBoxx $ Investment Grade Corporate Bond ETF (LQD) yields 3.32%. It's not quite the 4% that we're looking for. But when you consider that the iShares U.S. Treasury Bond ETF (GOVT) currently yields 1.96%, I think you'll agree that there's a case to be made for allocating at least a portion of your bond holdings to corporate bonds.

## Junk Bonds

The term "junk bond" is attached to non-investment grade issues. Naturally, a junk bond will pay a higher premium than an investment grade bond. Depending on your appetite for risk, it's not necessary to avoid these bonds altogether. The yields are exceptionally attractive, but also in line with the entailed risk. Just like with investment grade corporate bonds, we can mitigate the impact of a specific bond going into default by investing in an index. However, you're going to notice that an index of junk bonds is more volatile than an index of investment grade bonds. Junk bonds are prone to move in tandem with stocks, which differs from the movements of Treasuries and investment grade corporate bonds. This correlation should be considered when weighting the portfolio. A small junk bond allocation to accompany other bonds can serve as healthy diversification, while too much reliance on junk bonds will increase risk and fail to provide insulation when stocks decline. I recommend limiting your junk bond exposure to no more than 5% of the portfolio. It will provide an extra bump in terms of yield as well as some added diversification.

At the time of writing, the SPDR Bloomberg Barclays High Yield Bond ETF (JNK) yields 5.61%. This is the kind of bump we need. But keep in mind, when the inevitable pullback in the stock market arrives, junk bonds are likely to follow suit. Keep the allocation conservative and see things through as you continue to collect your distributions.

## REITs

REITs are an easy way to gain broad exposure to the real estate market. They provide room for both strong growth and high yields. It's an equity investment, so we should expect capital appreciation. In order to qualify as a REIT, the company must distribute 90% of their rental income to shareholders. As a result, your dividend is guaranteed (although the size of the dividend may fluctuate). With common stocks, the dividend is never guaranteed, though in many cases it's expected. This creates a unique disparity between common stocks and REITs. A publicly traded company has the option of either retaining all their income or making a distribution to shareholders. A REIT, on the other hand, is required to make a distribution. In many cases, what we end up seeing is larger capital gains from the stock market and stronger dividend yields from the REIT market.

Both of these markets should serve as constant staples in the portfolio. It's good diversification. But my advice is to overweight in favor of stocks during the early years (for growth), and then gradually shift the portfolio in favor of REITs in the later years (for yield).

At the time of writing, the Vanguard Real Estate Index Fund ETF Shares (VNQ) is yielding 3.29%. It doesn't currently deliver the 4% that we're after, but when you consider that the SPDR S&P 500 ETF (SPY) is only yielding 1.85%, a preference towards REITs in the later years makes sense.

## Mortgage REITs

It's important to note that there are two kinds of REITs: equity REITs and mortgage REITs. Equity REITs are the most common, and as the name implies, investors receive an ownership interest in the underlying properties. With a mortgage REIT, you're investing in a combination of residential and commercial mortgages. The purpose of the mortgage REIT is to provide liquidity to the real estate market, and this also provides investors with an opportunity to build a stream of dividend income. Both equity REITs and mortgage REITs are required to distribute 90% of their income to the shareholders. While both types of REITs are known for offering attractive yields, the yield on a mortgage REIT can be substantially higher, oftentimes reaching into the double digits.

At the time of writing, the VanEck Vectors Mortgage REIT Income ETF (MORT) is yielding 7.67%. In small increments, this will provide a nice boost to your dividend stream. But as a word of caution, mortgage REITs are riskier than equity REITs, hence the stronger yield. In a sense, they're the junk bonds of REITs. It's a form of debt rather than equity, and the yield is aligned with the level of risk that you assume. I recommend limiting exposure in mortgage REITs to no more than 5% of your portfolio.

## Dividend Aristocrats

It's unlikely that you'll achieve a 4% yield from the Dividend Aristocrats. It's not
an index of high yielding companies. Rather, it's an index of companies that consistently increase their dividends

(regardless of how small that dividend might be). But that doesn't mean the Dividend Aristocrats aren't an important addition to the portfolio, even in the later years when yield is important.

By definition, the Dividend Aristocrats is an index of companies belonging to the S&P 500 that have increased their dividend every year for at least the past 25 years. To be a constituent, the company must also have market capitalization of at least $3 billion. It's a high bar to hurdle, and a relatively finite group of companies manage to find a home in this index. What we get here is a form of distribution that functions very different from bond interest, and the accompanying benefit isn't recognized right away.

With bonds, the principal is relatively stagnant, and the yield is a product of what the Federal Open Market Committee decides to enact. As we've seen, during times of high inflation, rates might get up as high as 8% (in practice, there really isn't a ceiling, and it could conceivably go much higher). During times of economic recovery, interest rates can be cut to almost zero. Stock dividends are different. The underlying investment exhibits greater volatility. Where a $1,000 investment in bonds is likely to return $1,000 plus interest, the value of a stock is going to change (hopefully for the better), and this means that the yield is impacted.

If a stock appreciates in value, in order for the company to maintain their dividend yield (when expressed as a percent), they must increase the dollar amount of their dividend. But if a stock pays a $0.75 dividend before increasing in value and continues to pay $0.75 after increasing in value, it means that the yield has been reduced. This scenario isn't good for the ongoing valuation of the stock, and it's not good for the investor. *As dividend investors, we hope that the company increases their dividend as the value of the stock increases!*

When it comes to the Dividend Aristocrats, it's not so much about what the index is yielding today, but more so about the yield in relation to what you paid for the investment. If you place $1,000 in a fund of stocks that have a history of increasing their dividend every year, you can expect that the yield against the initial $1,000 investment will increase each year. In other words, your dividend payments, when expressed in dollars rather than percent, should keep getting bigger each and every year. And the $1,000 investment should appreciate along with it (though in some years we might experience a decline).

The same can't be said about our bond investment. If interest rates are 3%, then our $1,000 investment yields $30.00. If rates are cut to 2.50% by the time the bond matures, then the interest on our $1,000 will only be $25 (should we decide to reinvest).

That's the interesting thing about our "risk-free" investments—*their distributions can change at maturity, and not always for the better.* The $1,000 investment is viewed as safe, but who knows what rate we'll be able to reinvest it at? Over the long-haul, who knows what the distribution on Treasuries will look like? In my opinion, Treasuries provide greater risk than they get credit for.

If you invest in the Dividend Aristocrats, the value of the $1,000 will fluctuate, but the distribution is expected to increase each year. For the long-term investor, we anticipate that the $1,000 investment will appreciate over time, but it's an equity market, so it's possible that we'll encounter some rocky terrain along the way.

I'm not suggesting that you side with one investment over the other. Both play an important role in structuring a properly diversified portfolio. But when you get to retirement, you'll prefer safety and cash flow over growth. With Treasuries, the principal is safe but the distribution isn't. It can be jerked all over the place. With the Dividend Aristocrats, the principal will fluctuate, yet we expected the distribution to progressively increase. From my perspective, this means that the distribution is safer and less volatile than that of the Fed funds rate. If you want a sense of safety when it comes to both principal and distribution, hold both investments. The percent that you allocate to each is a matter of personal preference. Traditional investment advice is that you overweight in favor of Treasuries. The Dividend Aristocrats can then be added to ensure that a portion of your dividend income continues to increase each year.

At the time of writing, ProShares S&P 500 Dividend Aristocrats ETF (NOBL) is yielding 2.01%. But remember, we expect the dollar value of the distributions to increase each year. It's not the yield when calculated as a percent of the current value that's important; rather, it's the yield when calculated against what you paid for the investment that counts. This type of fund is a long-term holding that rewards patience in due time.

## Preferred Stock

Preferred stock is attractive to the investor seeking yield over growth. In fact, you'll get a stronger distribution with most preferred stock funds than you will with the S&P 500 or even the Dividend Aristocrats. This is because preferred stock funds tend to seek exposure from the higher yielding sectors, such as utilities, financials, energy, and telecom. The distribution from a preferred stock fund is therefore contingent on the distribution from the preferred shares of companies in these sectors. But the movement of preferred stocks is detached from the movement of common stocks.

In a sense, preferred shares function like debt rather than equity. Unlike common stock, issuers of preferred stock are required to meet their dividend payments. For this reason, the dividend is often higher, but the price is relatively stagnant.

Preferred shares are only issued to institutional buyers, meaning you can't just log in to your discount brokerage account and buy them up. What you can do is invest in an ETF that holds preferred stock in many companies. Given that there's safety in numbers, this is what we'd want to do anyways.

At the time of writing, the iShares Preferred Income Securities ETF (PFF) is yielding 5.59%. It's not expected to provide much in the way of appreciation, but it will provide a nice little kick to your dividend income. The yield is comparable to that of junk bonds and mortgage REITs, yet these types of investments are often stable with very little fluctuation. When cash distribution is the goal, it's prudent to allocate as much as 10% to 15% of the portfolio to a fund that represents the broader preferred stock market. This will go a long way towards achieving an overall portfolio yield of 4%.

**Gold**

As we know, gold does not pay a dividend. Instead, it provides an opportunity for growth when equities aren't doing their job. But come retirement, the focus changes. We want to maintain our holdings while collecting enough money to live on. This begs the question, do we need gold in retirement? And if so, how much?

If you're able to live off of your distributions while maintaining your exposure to gold, it's wise to do so. Over a 30 year retirement, you're likely to encounter multiple occasions when gold comes to the rescue. This is good for the portfolio, but it's not essential.

Remember, we want to own our age minus 10 years in bonds, but come retirement we might actually decide to put a cap on our bond exposure. Something along the lines of 50% is reasonable. If we hold our age minus ten years right up into our nineties, we won't be properly diversified and our portfolio yield will be at the discretion of the Federal Open Market Committee. With a 50% holding, our bond exposure will still be sizeable, meaning we'll have plenty of protection with or without gold. When equities take a hit, bonds will hold their ground. Some gold would be nice, but if you require a larger distribution, reducing your reliance on gold is an easy way to increase the stream of dividend income.

The gold allocation doesn't have to be reduced to zero, and you don't have to wait until you need the cashflow to make the change. If you're nearing retirement and gold is strong, take it as an opportune time to reduce your allocation. If you're roughly halfway through your retirement and gold really takes off, you might consider it a good time to sell.

Gold likes to play possum. It can perform poorly for the better part of a decade and then shoot for the stars. It's okay to go ahead and cash out when gold makes a run. You don't have to catch it at the very top. In fact, you probably won't. But if you bide your time and have patience, you can secure a handsome profit. Once this is done, reallocate the proceeds back into your other holdings and watch the dividend income increase.

**Stocks**

I saved the best, and most practical, for last. We've discussed stocks in terms of the Dividend Aristocrats and preferred stock. But when it comes to building a portfolio, we also need broad exposure to the greater market. For most, that means an allocation to SPDR S&P 500 ETF (SPY). This isn't going to earn a 4% dividend yield. In fact, at the time of writing, we're settling for 1.85%, so we're not even halfway there. This next bit of trivia might even sound depressing, but the last time the S&P 500 yielded more than 4% was in 1984, when inflation was high. *Ouch!* I'm not going to hold my breath waiting for that to happen again. There've been plenty of occasions since then when the yield got up over 3%. It's certainly not uncommon to see the yield exceed 2%. But when you get down to it, striving for a 4% yield on the portion of the portfolio dedicated to broad stock market exposure is simply unrealistic.

So, the real question is, *how much of your portfolio do you allocate to the S&P 500 come retirement?* The answer: *Not very much!*

What I'm going to say here goes against the grain of traditional investment advice. Even in retirement, most financial advisors will advocate investing the bulk of your equity allocation in the stock market while allocating a modest percent to REITs. And that's fine. It's acceptable to follow their advice, and really, there's no danger in doing so. But I'm going to encourage you to keep reading and hear my argument for favoring a higher allocation of REITs over stocks come retirement.

It's important to maintain exposure to both equity markets for the sake of diversification. And yes, even in our golden years, it's nice to have a healthy portion of capital appreciation to accentuate our dividend income. But what we really want are investments that provide strong and sustainable dividends. The S&P 500 may very well be our lowest yielding investment. That's okay, because we can keep the exposure to moderate proportions (somewhere between 5% and 10% of our holdings).

For starters, bonds will constitute about half of the portfolio. This leaves approximately 50% allocated amongst stocks, real estate, and however much you still want allocated to gold. If you choose to maintain a 10% gold allocation, then you have 40% remaining to allocate amongst equities. In addition to the S&P 500, this also includes your exposure to the Dividend Aristocrats, to preferred stocks, and to REITs.

As mentioned above, stocks provide stronger growth than REITs, but REITs are required to distribute 90% of their income as dividends. As a result, their yields are typically higher than that of the S&P 500. In our early investing years, we should favor stocks to REITs, but in the later income-dependent years, REITs provide the type of distribution that we're after. Again, we want to own both stocks and REITs at every point in the investment horizon, but the allocation should be adjusted as we progress towards retirement. Once retired, maybe we'll want to allocate 25% of the portfolio to REITs and split the remaining 15% between the S&P 500, Dividend Aristocrats, and preferred shares. Maybe we want to throw in a fund or two that tracks a high yielding sector, like utilities or telecom stocks. Or maybe the yield on bonds has dropped, and given the opportunity to sell our long-term bond funds at a gain, maybe we'll want to allocate a greater percent of the portfolio amongst equities. There's no golden rule and the economic environment is far from static. While I typically don't recommend adjusting the allocation based on the economic environment—*it should be adjusted based on age as you progress through your investment horizon*—I do advocate exceptions come retirement. At this stage, income is critical, as is safety. And when your stocks and bonds don't provide adequate yields, it makes sense to rearrange the portfolio based on desired yield, so long as you maintain diversification across different markets and only allocate a small portion of the portfolio to the riskier, but higher yielding, assets.

**So how much do I hold of each asset class?**

We know that holding your age in bonds is the traditional wisdom. The risk adverse investor might even go so far as to allocated his age minus 10 years to bonds. Treasuries should form the nucleus of the bond allocation, but exposure to corporate bonds can be added to increase yield with a correspondingly smaller increase to risk. And while different schools of thought provide differing perspectives, my preference is for long-term securities. They provide an interest rate premium, you'll earn a higher yield for accepting a longer duration, and they provide protection when interest rates are reduced. On the negative side, they lose value when interest rates rise. Once you're locked in, you're locked in. But that's okay, because part of our strategy is to allow markets to work through their cycles. When we cover rebalancing, we'll see that there's an advantage to holding assets that depreciate as others accelerate, so long as their movements are cyclical and their direction will eventually reverse.

It's okay to diversify into other funds that pay an interest rate premium. Junk bonds and mortgage REITs can be used to gain significantly higher yields, but should only be tolerated in small increments. Each should comprise no more than 5% of the portfolio, and if you're holding both, it's okay to scale back the allocation.

From there, it's a tug of war between stocks, real estate, and gold. As stated above, no more than 10% of the portfolio should be allocated to gold. If you need to increase the yield on your portfolio, reducing the exposure to gold is a great way to do it. On average, gold will lose value during the good times and then step in to hit a home run during the bad times. So keep your allocation conservative and just let it do what it does.

I have another tool that might help. It's called the *Dividend Income Calculator*, and it's included in the same download as the other tools. It should help you determine the amount of dividend income you can expect given the yields in different markets. All you have to do is enter the weight and yield of each asset class you're invested in, and the spreadsheet will provide the overall portfolio yield.

| Dividend Income Calculator | | | | |
|---|---|---|---|---|
| Portfolio Value: | 1,500,000 | | | |
| Asset Class | Ticker | Weight | Yield | Div Income |
| Treasuries | GOVT | 20.00% | 2.01% | 6,030 |
| Corproate Bonds | LQD | 15.00% | 3.43% | 7,718 |
| Junk Bonds | JNK | 5.00% | 5.59% | 4,193 |
| Mortgage REITs | MORT | 5.00% | 7.32% | 5,490 |
| S&P 500 | SPY | 5.00% | 1.85% | 1,388 |
| Dividend Aristocrats | NOBL | 10.00% | 2.01% | 3,015 |
| Preferred Stock | PFF | 10.00% | 5.78% | 8,670 |
| Equity REIT | VNQ | 25.00% | 3.47% | 13,013 |
| Gold | GLD | 5.00% | 0% | - |
| | | Annual Dividend Income: | | 49,515 |
| | | Portfolio Yield: | | 3.30% |

This example illustrates what a portfolio might yield today given a slightly aggressive allocation for a retiree. Bonds comprise 40% of the portfolio, with only 5% being allocated to junk bonds. The remaining 35% is kept safe with an allocation that favors Treasuries. Given the fact that the Treasury fund scarcely yields more than 2%, we can see that the bond allocation holds the portfolio back. The corporate bond fund pays a premium, and the extra dividend yield makes a difference. Junk bonds add a nice little punch. Same with our mortgage REIT. We enjoy the added yield, but shouldn't expect much in the way of appreciation, and we need to accept that there will be periods when these investments depreciate in value. In a down market, we shouldn't expect either security to perform well, but we also have 5% allocated to gold, so there's a hedge in place when our heavy hitters need to take a breather.

I've only allocated 5% to the S&P 500, and there's a good reason why. We're also holding the Dividend Aristocrats. We can expect capital appreciation from both funds, but the Dividend Aristocrats provides a better yield. In an up market, it's possible that the S&P 500 will outpace the Dividend Aristocrats. But in a down market, people seek the security of sustainable dividends, and for this reason, the Dividend Aristocrats generally take a smaller hit during recessions. While the size of their movements might differ, we still expect them to move roughly in the same direction. We expect these funds to exhibit strong positive correlation, so by holding both, we can view the pair as a full 15% allocation to the domestic stock market. At this stage, we also want to allocate 10% to preferred stock because of the impressive yield. And finally, we want REITs to outweigh our stock allocation, and we achieve that with a 25% allocation.

Of course, this isn't the only way to allocate a portfolio. While there are different conventions and schools of thought, it's impossible to say that there is a "right" way to allocate the portfolio.

The great thing about the spreadsheet is that you can develop different scenarios by changing the weights and yields. What would it look like if Treasuries yielded 3%, or even 4%, instead of 2%? Under such a scenario, we would also expect corporate bonds and junk bonds to provide higher yields. Would you allocate the portfolio any differently under such circumstances? What if we experience a crash and the Federal Open Market Committee cuts rates down to 0.5%? You'd probably wish you were holding more gold. But if you wait until after you wish you were holding gold to buy it, you're probably not going to get in at a lucrative price. That's why it's so important to allocate the portfolio appropriately and then stick to your plan.

As stated above, this allocation is aggressive for a retiree. It has a 50% equity allocation and 10% is being allocated to high risk, high yielding junk bond and mortgage REIT funds. But at the same time, it benefits from the interest rate premium that corporate bonds provide, and there's enough allocated to Treasuries that damage will be mitigated during a pullback, so long as our retiree doesn't panic and sell.

The real question is, can you survive off the 3.3% yield that this example provides? If it's more than you need, maybe you want to be more conservative and increase the bond allocation. Or maybe you want to live on less than what the portfolio yields and continually reinvest a portion of the dividends. These are safety measures that we can strive for. The bigger the portfolio, the easier it is to reinvest a portion of the earnings, and that's what want to do. Throughout our working years, we're striving to build a portfolio that provides autonomy. We want to be comfortable and then some. Striving for a 4% dividend yield helps. Given the right market conditions, it's very attainable. And in other markets, it's simply not. At any given time, there will be certain securities that yield more than 4%. If properly diversified, higher yielding securities can make a world of difference. But it's important not to take excessive risk in an effort to increase yield. We want proper representation from stocks, bonds, and real estate, while an allocation to gold can be maintained at the retiree's discretion.

In *Chapter 9: Benchmarking,* we'll discuss the process of tracking progress throughout our working years. Even if we can't rely on a consistent 4% yield come retirement, we can take steps to ensure that our retirement is comfortable. Perhaps we need to save more so that we can live on a smaller yield. Or perhaps we need to take advantage of the fact that the 4% rule was designed with the intention of eating into the principal. Getting to where we need to be should be a boring yet fulfilling ride.

Before we get too far ahead of ourselves, let's talk rebalancing. I keep mentioning it as though the process is common knowledge, and maybe it is. But if it's not, the next chapter will tell you everything you need to know.

# Chapter 7

## Rebalancing

We're finally here, the chapter where we see how a rebalancing strategy can assist us in (*almost*) always recognizing gains instead of losses. The bedrock, of course, is finding markets that have a history of beating inflation over the long-run, do not exhibit strong positive correlation, and then determining the percent of the portfolio we want to invest in each of these markets. Risk tolerance is different for everyone, but we'll proceed as though the right mix is what we discussed above—your age minus 10 years allocated to bonds, with the remainder divided between stocks, real estate, and gold. In the following examples, we'll assume a preference for stocks over real estate, knowing that this preference might change as we near retirement.

We'll start by keeping things simple. In the first example, we're only going to invest in one bond fund, one stock fund, one real estate fund, and gold.
In this example, our investor is 35 years old, has been building her portfolio since she graduated college some 12 years earlier, and has already accumulated $200,000 in wealth. Given that she'll want to allocate 25% of her holdings to bonds, her portfolio might be allocated as follows:

| Fund | Allocation | Weight |
|---|---|---|
| | | |
| Bonds | 50,000.00 | 25.00% |
| Stocks | 85,000.00 | 42.50% |
| Real Estate | 55,000.00 | 27.50% |
| Gold | 10,000 | 5.00% |
| | | |
| Total | 200,000.00 | |

Let's pretend that no additional capital is invested in the portfolio, and rather than receiving cash distributions, all dividends are automatically reinvested back into the fund that that they are paid from. Therefore, dividends will basically function as capital gains. With time, each fund will either increase in value or decrease in value. While it would be fun to watch all of our investments appreciate simultaneously, we have to accept that this will not always be the case, as short-term movements can go in either direction, and downturns can last anywhere from several months to upwards of a decade.

A year passes and our investor experiences a nice gain of 17.5% in her stock fund. The real estate market, however, did not perform well, and the fund decreased in value by 11.5%. She earned interest at a fixed rate of 2.25% on the bond fund, and with a fluctuation in value due to the Federal Open Market Committee increasing rates, the fund actually decreased in value by 2.5%, for an annualized loss of 0.25%. Gold did what we expect it to do when stocks perform well, and decreased by a modest 2%. Therefore, the value of her portfolio changes as follows:

| Fund | Allocation | Return | New Balance | Weight |
|---|---|---|---|---|
| | | | | |
| Bonds | 50,000.00 | -0.25% | 49,875.00 | 23.95% |
| Stocks | 85,000.00 | 17.50% | 99,875.00 | 47.96% |
| Real Estate | 55,000.00 | -11.50% | 48,675.00 | 23.38% |
| Gold | 10,000 | -2.00% | 9,800.00 | 4.71% |
| | | | | |
| Total | 200,000.00 | | 208,225.00 | |

On the plus side, she made money. An annual return of $8,225 on a $200,000 portfolio isn't huge, but the real estate market went into correction mode while an increase to the interest rate took a small toll on her bond fund. As a long-term investor, she should expect stronger returns in the future. Yet there's no guarantee of what her returns will look like over the next several years. Though money was made, the bond, real estate, and gold markets exhibited negative correlation with regard to the stock market, and as a result, the portfolio is no longer in balance.

Where 42.50% of the portfolio used to be allocated to stocks and 27.50% used to be allocated to real estate, she now has 47.96% allocated to stocks and 23.38% allocated to real estate. The percentages allocated to bonds and gold have hardly changed. If we round up slightly we could say that the allocations still rest at 25% and 5%, respectively. But our investor is now a year older, and therefore one year closer to retirement. She wants a bit more safety, which means that she should now allocate 26% of her portfolio to bonds.

*How is our investor going to get her asset allocation back on track?* The only way to get there is to sell some of the stock fund and invest the proceeds in the bond, real estate, and gold funds. For many investors, this approach will seem counterintuitive. *She did well with her stock investment, so why on earth would she want to sell some of it to invest in the real estate market (etc.), especially after she lost 11.5% on this investment?*

The truth is, the stock market will not trend upward indefinitely. It will eventually encounter some sort of correction, *or even a crash*. By selling enough stocks to get her portfolio back in balance, our investor recognizes some of her gains. If stocks continue to go up the following year, and perhaps continue to outperform bonds, real estate, and gold, our investor will sell even more of her stock fund in order to again reinvest in these other markets. She's not trying to predict the top of the market and sell all of her stocks at once. Instead, she'll continue to rebalance her portfolio at least annually, and this will force her to progressively take more and more gains from her stock fund as the market approaches its top. When it finally falls, the rebalancing strategy will then force her to sell shares from whatever markets are performing well, and she'll reinvest the proceeds back into stocks because market conditions have forced the price lower. After having rebalanced for the stock gains that she recognized upon turning 36, the pie will be a tad larger, and by increasing the bond allocation to 26%, it will also be a tad safer.

To continue, let's say that over the next year, we get a stock market correction, causing her fund to decline by 12.5%. Adding insult to injury, the performance of the real estate market is lackluster, and we see gains of only 1.5%, mainly because the fund continued to receive rents while property values declined. Our bond fund, however, did its job. Interest payments came in at 2.5% while the fund rose in value by 0.75%, providing for a combined return of 3.25%. And gold packed the punch we expect it to pack, it rose in value by a whopping 22%. By the time our investor turns 37, her portfolio will be as follows:

| Fund | Allocation | Return | New Balance | Weight |
|---|---|---|---|---|
| | | | | |
| Bonds | 49,875.00 | 3.25% | 51,495.94 | 24.73% |
| Stocks | 99,875.00 | -12.50% | 87,390.63 | 41.97% |
| Real Estate | 48,675.00 | 1.50% | 49,405.13 | 23.73% |
| Gold | 9,800 | 22.00% | 11,956.00 | 5.74% |
| | | | | |
| Total | 208,225.00 | | 200,247.69 | |

Again, the performance isn't impressive. In fact, our investor lost just about everything she made during the prior year. But it's important to note that the results could have been worse. Remember, at the end of the prior year, she sold some of the stock fund to buy more bonds, real estate, and gold. If she hadn't rebalanced her portfolio, the decline would have hit her a lot harder. She'd have been more heavily invested in the stock fund, which lost value, and not as heavily invested in the real estate fund, which had a slight increase. We also see the benefit that gold adds. It won't always increase in value, but when it packs a punch, it packs a punch.

During the first year, the process of rebalancing forced our investor to chip away at her gains as she reinvested the proceeds in the losing (or discounted) funds. There is indeed a benefit to rebalancing, and our investor does not need to predict market direction in order to recognize this benefit. She simply needs to continue with her rebalancing strategy, so long as she's invested in the right markets.

Over a prolonged investment span, our investor can expect her average returns to exceed what is illustrated here. It all comes down to the fact that markets move in cycles. If our investor rebalances her portfolio as her different holdings progress through their cycles, she'll do much better than she would by simply buying each of her holdings and not touching them again until retirement. That's the power of rebalancing. And when used in conjunction with compounded dividends, the portfolio is destined to succeed.

I've provided another tool to help manage your portfolio. It's called the Portfolio Rebalancing Calculator. This will help you determine the number of shares for each security that need to be bought and sold when you rebalance. Just like before, enter the required information in the yellow cells, and the results will calculate for you.

**Portfolio Rebalancing Calculator**

Commission per trade 4.95 Cost to rebalance 49.50

| Ticker | Target Weight | Beginning Shares | Price Per Share | Beginning Value | Actual Weight | Weight Variance | Shares to Buy / (Sell) | Ending Share Total | Ending Value | Ending Weight |
|---|---|---|---|---|---|---|---|---|---|---|
| SPY | 20% | 30 | 260.92 | 7,827.60 | 8% | -12% | 48 | 78 | 20,351.76 | 20% |
| NOBL | 10% | 185 | 61.98 | 11,466.30 | 11% | 1% | (22) | 163 | 10,102.74 | 10% |
| VGK | 10% | 250 | 50.37 | 12,592.50 | 12% | 2% | (49) | 201 | 10,124.37 | 10% |
| VPL | 10% | 100 | 63.30 | 6,330.00 | 6% | -4% | 60 | 160 | 10,128.00 | 10% |
| VNQ | 15% | 200 | 78.94 | 15,788.00 | 16% | 1% | (7) | 193 | 15,235.42 | 15% |
| VNQI | 5% | 95 | 54.65 | 5,191.75 | 5% | 0% | (2) | 93 | 5,082.45 | 5% |
| REM | 5% | 25 | 42.29 | 1,057.25 | 1% | -4% | 91 | 116 | 4,905.64 | 5% |
| BND | 15% | 260 | 79.27 | 20,610.20 | 20% | 5% | (68) | 192 | 15,219.84 | 15% |
| BNDX | 5% | 130 | 54.40 | 7,072.00 | 7% | 2% | (37) | 93 | 5,059.20 | 5% |
| EDV | 5% | 75 | 111.74 | 8,380.50 | 8% | 3% | (30) | 45 | 5,028.30 | 5% |
| Cash | | | | 5,000.00 | | | | | 28.88 | |
| | | | | | | | | | | |
| Total | 100% | | | 101,316.10 | | | | | 101,266.60 | 100% |

## *So that's the strategy!*

There you have it. That's our strategy. You've seen how it works, and I hope you agree that it's so simple that anyone can implement the strategy. We're simply going to invest in funds that provide broad exposure to the stock, real estate, bond, and gold markets. As we gain experience and become more sophisticated investors, we'll add other funds to the mix in order to improve diversification and increase dividend yield. But when you look at the core of our strategy, holding just four broad market funds is sufficient. We're going to buy into them every month with the same amount of money, and we'll do so regardless of what the markets have done or what we think they might do next. By doing so, we obtain lucrative prices, because more shares are purchased when markets dip. The average price paid per share will be less than the average price that the shares have sold for. And when markets are priced below their moving average, there's no harm in tightening our budget in order to throw some extra cash into the portfolio.

The portfolio will be allocated based on our tolerance for risk, with the percent allocated to bonds increasing gradually over time. We'll see that our portfolio falls out of balance. Some funds will increase in value as others decline. We must therefore rebalance the portfolio, which is a process that serves two distinct purposes: (1) it realigns the portfolio with our tolerance for risk, and (2) it forces us to sell high and buy low in a systematic manner. There's no need to predict market direction.

We also want to reinvest all of our dividend income. This allows us to build the portfolio, perpetually increasing the number of shares that dividends are paid against. The goal is to earn dividend income on top of our reinvested divided income, and then repeat the process.

Of course, how we invest our funds is only the second part of the equation. The first part is about budgeting and saving. When you get down to it, it's about lifestyle and the ability to live below your means. That's the most important ingredient when it comes to achieving financial independence. Investing the right way gives you an extra edge and it prevents you from incurring large losses, but it's not a substitute for saving. The earlier you start saving, the better off you'll be. And the more that you're able to save each month, the quicker your portfolio will grow. From there, markets provide the returns that they provide. Your job is to ride the wave, reinvest your dividends, and use your rebalancing strategy to gain an extra advantage.

*Simple, right? Of course it is!* But it's not just simple, it's also effective.

I wouldn't be doing my job if I didn't explain why it's effective. I also wouldn't be doing my job if you don't walk away from *Preparing For Financial Success* with a thorough understanding of why this approach works better than picking our own stocks.

Remember our friends from the cocktail party? They're always picking their own stocks and they're always bragging about their conquests. We've never heard them talk about a losing investment. But that's okay. They seem to know what they're doing, so they probably don't have very many losers to talk about.

*Let's find out what the founders of our investment approach think about our friends!*

# Chapter 8

## Why it Works

Most new investors are surprised to learn that investing isn't necessarily about picking stocks. Unless you're flipping houses or buying rental properties, picking stocks might actually seem like the only other way to invest. It's all they talk about on CNBC. It's what Jim Cramer builds his show around. And when you get down to the fundamentals of what a stock represents, it makes sense that they're the driving force behind the market. A strong economy is going to be reflected in strong companies, and it's the companies that provide a needed product or service in an efficient manner that are destined to lead the pack. But to invest successfully, you don't need to hone some special skill aimed at identifying the next successful company before it takes off. And you're likely to do better if you don't even try.

Don't get me wrong, picking stocks can be a lot of fun. *If you enjoy it, do it!* But treat it as a hobby. Take it out of the 30% of your budget that is allocated to wants. When it comes to retirement savings, betting your future on hand-selected companies is a risky game. Hold the market. Hold multiple markets. And make sure that the markets you're invested in all have a history of beating inflation when invested in for extended periods of time. It might sound redundant at this point, *but it works!* And the reason why it works is called the efficient market hypothesis.

According to the hypothesis, when markets behave as efficiently as they should, the only way to profit from picking individual stocks is to either receive inside information or, for the law-abiding citizen, just get plain old lucky.

Most of us don't work for a hedge fund or analyze stocks for a living. We have other endeavors that consume our days, and varying responsibilities that eat into our evenings and weekends. But while we're getting on with life, the financial analysts are researching securities around the clock. They work incredibly long hours and endure tremendous stress . . . *all in hopes of beating the market!*

For every credible stock, bond, or commodity in existence, there's a host of financial analysts working tiresome hours in an effort know everything there is to know about it. According to the Bureau of Labor Statistics, there were 296,100 financial analysts employed in the United States in 2016, and the 10 year outlook indicates that the profession will grow by 10%. So if there are more than 296,100 financial analysts out there dedicating themselves 100% to picking (*hopefully*) winning investments, *what information about a stock are you going to gather over the weekend that these people don't already know?* In all likelihood, nothing. You can do all the research you want. *But can the hobbyist really expect to learn something about a security that isn't already known?*

The analysts are working for hedge funds, mutual funds, and other institutional investors. These entities buy and sell stocks in extremely large quantities, and that's what determines the price. When they buy, the price goes up. When they sell, the price goes down. This happens all while the individual investor buys and sells at whatever price is being offered. The result is that every bit of information that the financial analyst can gather about a stock is automatically factored into its price.

This is the basis behind the efficient market hypothesis. The hypothesis was developed by Nobel Prize in Economics winner Eugene Fama. His argument is that stocks always trade at their fair value, and this makes it impossible for investors to purchase stocks at a discount and later sell them at a premium. Instead, we purchase them at a fair price, and when we're ready to sell, we hope that something has happened to the stock that will make the fair price higher than what it was when we bought it. In order for the price to move in either direction, there must be some sort of news release that changes the analyst's evaluation of the stock, and this change will be immediately factored into the price. This makes it impossible to consistently outperform the stock market by selecting your own portfolio of stocks. There is no amount of research that allows one investor to gain an edge over the other investors. Our investor can't even gain an advantage by listening to an earnings call or being the first to read a news release. All of the financial analysts are listening and reading along with him, and the new information immediately goes into the price of the stock.

In practice, it can be argued that the efficient market hypothesis holds true most of the time. But there have been, and certainly will be again, market conditions where investor behavior is truly irrational, and the price of stocks and other securities do not reflect that of an efficient market. The financial crisis of 2008 is a prime example. The stock market saw losses of greater than 7% on certain days, intermixed with gains of greater than 10% on other days. And though the news was gloomy, there were no abrupt changes in the news to validate a 10% jump immediately after a 7% fall, let alone a series of these schizophrenic movements. People were making investment decisions based on fear and greed, and the market didn't know how to price itself. The "sideways" market that followed the 10% stock market correction in February 2018 is another great example. News coverage kept us up to date on escalating trade tension, rapid currency devaluation in Turkey, extreme budget deficits in Italy, and predictions that the US interest rate will continually ease upwards over an extended period of time. Yet the markets couldn't digest this news and pick a direction. The volatility lasted greater than ten months, but with all of these up and down movements, the market really did nothing more than move sideways. Even John Bogle, the father of index fund investing, said he'd never seen anything like it in all his years as an investor.

It can be argued that these conditions create market timing opportunities and that quick and substantial profits can be made. It can also be argued that anyone making these profits got lucky. Volatility does create the opportunity to get in and out of a stock at substantially different prices in a relatively short period of time. But it's important to remember that just because markets are volatile doesn't mean they're going to move in your favor. It simply means that markets have been experiencing broad movements, and there's no exact science to predicting whether the next movement will be up or down. For every buyer there has to be a seller, and this indicates that someone has guessed right on every trade. It also indicates that someone has guessed wrong on every trade. Academic studies have shown that those who guess right are likely to get overconfident and continue guessing, and their chances of consistently guessing right diminish over time.

The efficient market hypothesis does not mean that buying one stock is just as good as buying another. Yes, under normal market conditions, the hypothesis states that all known information is priced into each stock, and therefore all stocks are fairly priced. But simply buying one stock and concluding that it's the same as having bought any other stock would be incorrect. News about one stock could be substantially different from news about the others. One investment could move sideways for months while others become worthless. Or maybe one of them will gradually increase in value with returns that scarcely beat the rate of inflation, while yet another stock heads for the moon. We'll never know in advance because we can't predict the future. That's why we don't want to include individual stocks in our retirement accounts. If we do, it should be a very small holding, nothing greater than 5%. It's easier to invest in the entire stock market, and the long-term results are more predictable . . . *and boring!*

The stock market, when invested in as a whole, is a sure bet. It's like walking into a casino where the odds are stacked in the player's favor. The only caveat is that you have to let the money ride for the long-run.

I hope the hypothesis seems simple, because it is. In fact, most aspects of modern investing are simple. We have tools at our disposal that older generations weren't privy to. The index fund didn't come into existence until John Bogle launched the Vanguard First Index Investment Trust in 1976. It tracked the S&P 500, and at the time, this was the only index that could be purchased through a single security. Today we have hundreds of index funds at our disposal and we don't have to pay large commissions to buy them.

Everyone has access to a selection of online discount brokers, and this means we can build our own portfolios as we execute orders for as little as $4.95. This convenience hasn't always existed.

In my opinion, today is one of the best times in history to be an investor. It's not because we've experienced a 10 year bull run and markets can only go higher. The reality of the situation is that we have no idea where markets will go next. We have a lot of naysayers predicting that we're overdue for a bear market. But still, it's one of the best times to be an investor because we have the tools and the theories that are needed to get the job done. We don't have to pay expensive commissions or buy expert advice. All we need is a discount broker, some index funds, and an understanding of how markets work. From there, the world is our oyster.

But just because Eugene Fama gave us a theory doesn't mean the theory doesn't have critics. In fact, there are plenty of counter arguments. For starters, if markets are efficient, how can we have herd mentality? Think about it. If all information that is known about a security is already factored into the price, how is it that herd behavior can take over and change the short-term direction of the market?

*It's a reasonable question, isn't it?*

If Eugene Fama is telling us that everything that can be known about a security is already factored into the price, how can herd behavior push markets to dangerously high levels? And how can those markets eventually crash without a corresponding news release to substantiate markets suddenly being valued 30% lower than they were the day before?

The truth is, markets aren't always efficient. They're efficient until the herd takes over, and then they're irrational. So, if we can't beat the analysts by doing our own research when markets are efficient, how good are we going to be at picking stocks when markets behave irrationally?

If you've been paying attention then you already know my answer. I never try to call a top. If markets are irrationally high, my approach is to continue dollar cost averaging into each of the asset classes I'm invested in, and I make it a point to rebalance in conjunction with my predetermined schedule. It's when at least one of the markets we're invested in is irrationally high that the benefits of rebalancing shine the brightest.

When markets are irrationally low, I do the same. Except this time around, I try to throw some extra money into the pot. As I've said before, it's really difficult to call a top, but it's extremely easy to identify markets that are underpriced. So when markets are irrationally low, go ahead and buy a little extra. If they don't go up right away and become even more underpriced, go ahead and buy some more. As long as you have time on your side, you're going to come out ahead.

Investing doesn't have to be difficult. Our friends at the cocktail party might make it sound glamorous, but Eugene Fama makes it sound really, really boring. Between you and me, he's the guy I'm listening to. Nice, boring, easy, and effective. That's what I look for in an investment strategy.

And you know what? The boredom doesn't have to stop here. Let's dive a little deeper into theory. Eugen Fama isn't the only economists to have shaped investment strategy.

Nobel Prize winner Harry Markowitz also has some keen insight.

**Modern Portfolio Theory**

As investors, we know our goal is to achieve the highest possible return for our given tolerance for risk. But we have yet to truly define tolerance for risk. We know that it has something to do with increasing our bond exposure as we age, but how exactly do we define it? And how do we construct an entire portfolio around it?

In order to develop a deeper appreciation for risk management, we need to gain an understanding of modern portfolio theory. The theory first came to fruition in 1952 when economist Harry Markowitz published a paper titled *Portfolio Selection* in the Journal of Finance. His theory caught attention and is still taught in MBA programs all over the country.

We already know that risky assets are priced to provide larger returns than non-risky assets. If they weren't, no one would buy them. But Markowitz conveys that it doesn't matter how risky an asset is on its own, but rather how your portfolio can be expected to behave as different assets are combined.

I've stressed throughout the book that being diversified within a market is not enough. We need to be diversified across markets. There are, of course, terms for this concept. They're known as systematic risk and unsystematic risk.

Systematic risk, or market risk, is risk that's difficult to diversify away. It's pertains to an entire market. For example, when the Federal Open Market Committee votes to increase the interest rate, just about every domestic bond fund is going to take a hit. It doesn't matter how many bond funds you own, you can't diversify away this type of risk . . . *or can you?* Certain stock sectors, such as financial institutions, industrial companies, and energy providers, tend to perform well when interest rates rise. So if you also hold an ETF concentrated in one of these sectors, you've mitigated the impact of rising interest rates. But in all likelihood the mitigation is small. Most investors aren't too heavily invested in any one of these specific sectors. If the economic event were to be a recession rather than an interest rate hike, it's possible that everything would initially go down (but we're going to keep our fingers crossed that gold will pull through and pack a pretty strong punch). As I stated, systematic risk is difficult to diversify away. And in some economic environments, it's next to impossible.

Unsystemic risk, also known as specific risk, is the easiest risk to diversify away. This is the risk that's applicable to a specific company, or even a specific commodity, like gold. I provided an earlier example with REITs. Even when the real estate market is performing well, it's likely that certain REITs are being poorly managed and losing money. We don't have to branch into other markets to mitigate this type of risk. We simply need to hold many, many REITs. This is where the index fund comes into play.

Modern portfolio theory is all about combining assets to mitigate risk. As stated before, stocks, bonds, real estate, and gold all have a history of beating inflation when invested in for prolonged periods of time, yet each of these asset classes comes with inherent risk. If we hold all four asset classes, as opposed to investing in a single market, we reduce our risk but maintain our returns.

Diversification is the age-old method used to protect ourselves from losses. We aren't concerned with how our holdings behave individually; rather, we're concerned with how each asset interacts with the rest of the portfolio. Yet the assets are priced according to how they behave individually, not according to how they compliment each other. This is why the fully diversified investor has an advantage over the stock picker.

What we're really talking about is the concept of correlation. We don't want to invest in markets that always move in the same direction at the same time. With the modern portfolio theory, we're able to apply a mathematical framework to this objective.

Correlation can be measured in statistical terms on a scale from -1 to +1, with -1 signifying perfect negative correlation and +1 signifying perfect positive correlation. In the middle of these ranges is non-correlation, which is measured on a scale of -0.3 to +0.3. Anything between -1 and -0.3 exhibits negative correlation, assets measured between -0.3 to +0.3 are said not to be correlated, and anything above +0.3 is said to be positively correlated.

This helps set parameters. There's a range over which assets exhibit negative correlation, a range where they are said not to be correlated, and a range where they are said to be positively correlated.

While negative correlation might sound attractive from a hedging perspective, it won't provide a benefit. If two markets are negatively correlated, it means that more often than not, they will be moving in different directions. This is good from a safety perspective. As one asset goes down, another goes up, and this hedges our bets as the dividend income comes rolling in. But we've already seen what growth can do for a portfolio, and we know that the bigger the pie, the bigger the dividend distribution. It's extremely difficult to find two asset classes that are both going to beat inflation over periods of 20 to 40 years, yet will move in opposite directions more often than they move in the same direction. So what we really want are asset classes that not only beat inflation, but can do so while exhibiting very low levels of positive correlation. When this cannot be achieved, we will settle for assets that only exhibit moderate levels of positive correlation.

The below chart provides a visualization of what we're looking for. It compares the performance of five different funds over the 10 year recovery period that followed the 2008 financial crisis.

SPY – SPDR S&P 500 ETF
VNQ – Vanguard Real Estate Index Fund ETF
GLD – SPDR Gold ETF
EDV – Vanguard Extended Duration Treasury Index Fund ETF
JNK – SPDR Bloomberg Barclays High Yield Bond ETF

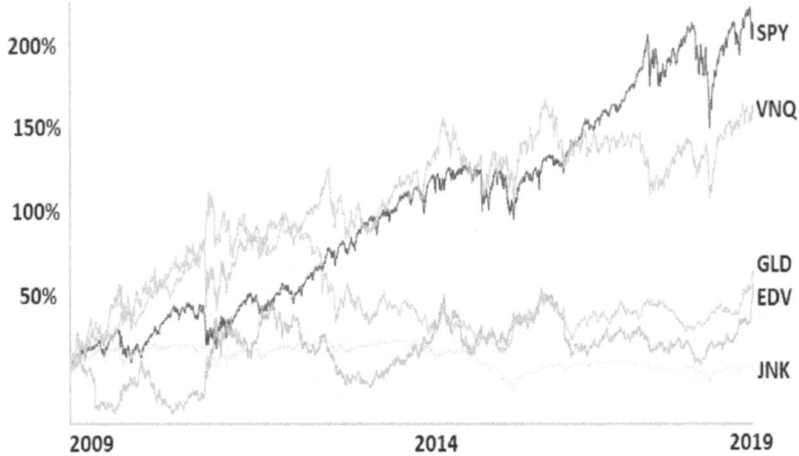


This is exactly what we want. With the exception of our junk bond holding, all funds increased in value over the 10 year period. The junk bond fund stayed relatively stagnant, but still ended lower than where it started. This is still okay, because it should be a small part of the portfolio—*that, and it pays a whopping dividend!*

What's truly important is as funds move higher, some move up above others and then later fall back below them. The long-term Treasury fund crosses the junk bond fund several times, because long-term bond holdings are more susceptible to changes in interest rates. Gold moves to the head of the pack in the early years, then falls behind. And while stocks are currently in the lead, they too crossed paths with both gold and real estate on multiple occasions.

*What does this mean?*

It means that there's a benefit to rebalancing because the assets classes do not consistently exhibit strong positive correlation. When gold took the lead, the act of rebalancing would have forced us to sell gold and buy into other funds. After gold fell back below stocks and real estate, the act of rebalancing would force us to recognize gains on our equities as we buy more gold (in other words, the act of rebalancing doesn't just secure gains, it gets us ready for the next recession).

Even junk bonds provide a benefit. Though relatively stagnant, when an asset class advances, we recognize gains and buy more junk bonds. When the asset class declines, we sell junk bonds and buy more of the other asset class. The back and forth is most obvious when comparing junk bonds to long-term Treasuries, but this benefit also applies to stocks, real estate, and gold. They may have moved higher up on the chart, but they still experience swings that force them to rebalance in conjunction with all of the other asset classes.

By diversifying into different markets that do not consistently exhibit strong positive correlation, what we truly want to achieve is the highest possible return for our accepted tolerance for risk. In order to do so, Markowitz gives us what is known as the efficient frontier.

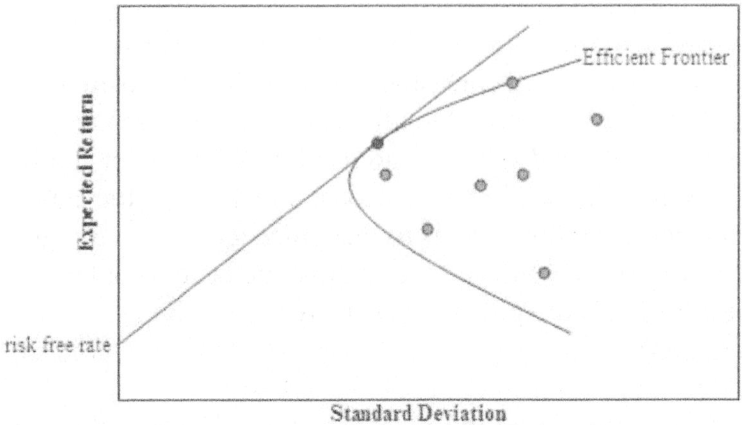


The efficient frontier depicts the expected return on the vertical axis and the standard deviation on the horizontal access. The slanted line represents the full spectrum of risky investments, where the risk-free asset at the bottom left would be a short-term Treasury, and as we progress upwards along the slant, assets of increasing risk fall along the line. The upper right extension of the line could conceivably represent Bitcoin or any number of penny stocks. Dots are plotted throughout what is known as the "risk-expected return space", representing portfolios of various risk. Every possible combination of assets can be plotted in this space, and the collection of all such possible portfolios defines a region in this space. The further below the frontier curve that a portfolio lies, the weaker its return relative to risk. A portfolio lying on the efficient frontier represents the combination offering the best possible expected return for the given tolerance for risk. A portfolio above the curve is theoretically impossible, though can be achieved when markets behave irrationally. Under normal market conditions, a security situated above the curve would represent an arbitrage opportunity, and when such opportunities arise, they are quickly exploited and dissolve. In other words, herd mentality will prevent portfolios from moving above the efficient frontier, so long as the herd behaves rationally.

It should be noted that there is no optimal point on the frontier curve. A young professional is likely to desire more risk than a retiree, and would therefore select a portfolio further to the upper right, where our retiree would prefer a portfolio somewhere along the lower left.

For each security, the standard deviation is synonymous with risk. The goal, therefore, is to combine assets that we expect to provide superior returns in such a manner that the portfolio standard deviation is reduced. The lower the correlation, the lower the standard deviation.

The fact that the frontier curves is significant. This shows how diversification improves the portfolio's risk and reward profile. It also indicates that the return diminishes as we assume more risk. It’s not a perfectly linear relationship. We reach the point where additional risk isn’t reciprocated with an equivalent increase in return. At some point, the overall expected return of the portfolio reduces as we continue adding more risk. Finding the right balance is critical to success.

I know what you must be thinking. The theory makes perfect sense. But how do I apply it? How do I ensure that my portfolio rests along the efficient frontier? You can buy software aimed at constructing efficient portfolios. And a good financial advisor can get you really close to where you want to be. But the truth is, you'll never maintain a portfolio that sits perfectly on the frontier for years on end.

It all comes down to the fact that correlations aren't static. Sometimes stocks and real estate show positive correlation for an entire decade, and then out of nowhere they show signs of negative correlation, or just stop being correlated whatsoever. Maybe a new tax law will give stocks a healthy boost while real estate flounders. *And nobody saw it coming!*

Other times, herd mentality changes. For whatever reason, the herd used to be bullish on both stocks and real estate, but a new report on climate change now has the herd uncertain about which real estate markets to invest in, so they're jumping ship in favor of tech companies that hold a bunch of digital real estate . . . and the rest of the stock market just keeps following the tech sector higher and higher.

The herd is a powerful force. It can disrupt an efficient market and it can abruptly change how closely two different asset classes are correlated. That's why modern portfolio theory is exactly what that name implies—*a theory!* We understand what the efficient frontier is, but it's difficult to develop a barometer that will tell us if we're exactly on it. And when our barometer gets us close, the environment is likely to change.

So they need to keep updating that software. Or your financial advisor needs to keep tweaking her model. And that's fine. If we're going to pay for advice, we want advice that's current. But is there a cheaper way to get the job done?

I like the do-it-yourself mentality because it keeps fees low, and with low fees, you have more funds to invest. In the long-run, I think we're all better off this way, as long as we implement an acceptable model. It doesn't have to be perfect, just accurate enough that we wouldn't be better off paying high fees for professional assistance. Or put more simply, it's okay to stray from the efficient frontier so long as it costs you less than the amount of money you would have paid a professional to get you closer.

The adage that investors should own their age in bonds is a quick and dirty rule aimed at moving your portfolio along the efficient frontier as your risk tolerance decreases. My preference for owning your age minus 10 years in bonds is an effort to keep the portfolio further up the right-hand side of the efficient frontier. Dividing the remainder of the portfolio amongst stocks, real estate, and gold moves the portfolio even closer to where we want to be.

If too much effort (and money) is invested in getting the portfolio as close as possible to the frontier, the benefit will dissolve. The efficient market hypothesis tells us that all information that is known about a security is already factored into the price. The price isn't going to change until something happens and is reported. If we take this concept a step further, correlation is the product of all that is known about two distinct assets. We can measure their past correlation, but we can't predict their future correlation. This means that we know where the efficient frontier was, which is different from knowing where it is. When correlation is slow to change, so is the efficient frontier. When it changes abruptly, the efficient frontier follows suit.

My preference is for the quick and dirty approach that keeps fees low. I start with my age minus 10 years in bonds. I allocate no more than 10% of the portfolio to gold as a means of hedging my equity investments. With the remainder, I hold more stocks than real estate in my working years, with a gradual shift to real estate as I approach the age where I will rely on the dividend income.

Efforts to further diversify should be conservative. The junk bond allocation, if desired, should be kept small. The same applies to mortgage REITs. These guys pay great dividends and are excellent tools both for building and providing cash flow. But we saw in the above example that a junk bond can gradually trend down without experiencing a recovery, even when the fund is held for 10 years. That's why we keep the allocation small and rebalance.

Whether you build the portfolio yourself or with an advisor, you want to be comfortable with the holdings. The self-directed investor who starts from scratch at a young age has many years to become comfortable with the approach while working with small amounts of money. It's the process of surviving market pullbacks and building the portfolio into something that's worth substantially more than the sum of what's been contributed that builds the confidence required to manage your wealth through retirement.

# Chapter 9

## Benchmarking

The objective of *Preparing For Financial Success* is about more than just setting a goal, developing conservative lifestyle habits, and then implementing an investment strategy. We also need to measure performance and, should we fall behind, make adjustments along the way.

Yes, we've developed a game plan. We've estimated the amount of wealth we need to accumulate, broken it down in terms of how much we'll need to contribute each month, and formulated an investment strategy that stacks the odds of achieving success in our favor. The only thing left to do is develop some benchmarks.

When it comes to your goal, lifestyle habits, and investment strategy, you're likely to develop a style that's all your own. The things in life that are important to you will differ from that of the next investor. And so too will your approach to portfolio construction. But when it comes to benchmarking, we all have one thing in common—*we need to meet our benchmarks, and we'll be better off if we exceed them!* If we fail in this area, then it's time to re-evaluate the budgeting and investing regimens that we've implemented.

The most common form of benchmarking is to measure the performance of your investments against the market average. A stock investor will likely measure the performance of their picks against the S&P 500, or perhaps a different benchmark suited to their approach, say a value index, an emerging market index, or even the S&P 500 Dividend Aristocrats index. It all depends on the type of stocks they invest in. A real estate investor is likely to measure the performance of their REITs against the Dow Jones U.S. Real Estate Index. It's likely that they'll also keep an eye on a stock index because they'll want to gauge whether or not real estate is keeping pace with other markets.

Unlike stock and real estate investors, bond investors face less uncertainty with their holdings. They know what the going rate of interest is when they purchase a bond, so measuring performance is less of an issue. Their primary concern is whether or not the interest payments will be honored, and so long as they hold the bond to maturity, fluctuations in the value of the bond are irrelevant. But for those trying to time the market and profit from selling bonds as interest rates decrease, measuring performance against a benchmark is a necessity. The difference between the stock investor who strives to beat the market and the bond investor with the same modus operandi is that the stock investor is searching for companies that are situated to provide superior performance, where the bond investor is attempting to time changes in the interest rate.

Of course, we're not trying to do any of these things. We're investing primarily in index funds. So by definition, our investments keep pace with their indexes. It makes sense to occasionally verify that each fund is indeed keeping pace. But aside from that, the index fund investor is concerned with whether or not he's selected the right markets to invest in, and given his tolerance for risk, whether or not he's allocated an appropriate proportion of the portfolio to each market.

Ultimately, the goal isn't to beat some easily replicated index each year. That game is better left to the stock pickers and market timers. Instead of benchmarking our performance against the S&P 500, what we really want to do is benchmark the value of our portfolio against the amount of money that we aim to accumulate at various stages in life.

I've stressed before that the amount of savings you come up with is far more important than how well you invest the savings. It's impossible to supplement a lack of savings by chasing after unrealistic returns. We could put $500 in a stock that beats the S&P 500 year after year, but if we never contribute more than $500 we'll never reach retirement. So what we need to start with is a benchmark for how much we plan to contribute to the portfolio each year, and then we'll strive to beat that benchmark.

We also have an affinity for dividends. Like other investors, we should be concerned with how much wealth we've accumulated at various stages in life. But as dividend investors we also need a benchmark for how much dividend income we're earning at each of those stages.

Aside from whether or not our investments performed as well as the appropriate index, we're generally concerned with three key benchmarks: (1) how much we contribute each year, (2) our stream of passive dividend income (including interest and rents), and (3) the balance of our portfolio at the end of each year.

Let's take a closer look at each of these benchmarks.

## Contribution

The first benchmark is simple. *Did we meet our savings goal and contribute as much capital to the portfolio as we were supposed to?* This is the easiest benchmark to control. The lifestyle we live is entirely up to us. And it's important to understand the difference between living as though you've accumulated wealth and actually living so that you can accumulate wealth.

In *Chapter 2: Budgeting* we talked about budgeting for the items that are truly important to us, and then doing our best not to spend money on things that aren't important. We're all going to incur luxury expenses of one form or another. These are the wants that make life worth living. But remember, our benchmarks are a top priority. If you're not meeting the first benchmark, then it's time to take a closer look at the budget. Were you able to follow the 50 / 30 / 20 rule (or perhaps a stricter rule that you set for yourself based on your retirement goal)? And if not, what can you cut back on in order to meet this benchmark without sacrificing too heavily from the life you want to live?

## Dividend Income

Our ultimate goal is to accumulate sufficient dividend income to live on. But it's not just an end goal. We also know that dividends provide the benefit of compounding. We use them throughout our investment horizon to build. And when markets perform poorly, we love the insulation they provide.

In terms of a benchmark, we need to ask ourselves, did the markets we're invested in provide the amount of dividend income we expect? If not, is it because they yielded less than expected? Or did we miss the first benchmark and not contribute enough capital?

The dividend benchmark is calculated based on an anticipated yield, but what we're really interest in is dollars, not the percent. The dollars generated each year will increase as we contribute more capital, reinvest our dividends, recognize capital gains, and rebalance the portfolio. As time passes we're going to shift from investments geared towards growth into investments that pay larger dividends. With time, we strive to build a stream of income that we can live from. But we're still going to measure the dollars at each stage of our investment horizon, not just for purposes of compounding, but for purposes of knowing what kind of income the portfolio can generate without sacrificing any of the shares should it become necessary to spend the income earlier than anticipated.

We'll also see that during a pullback there's a psychological benefit to counting our dividends. Unlike capital gains, dividends are always positive. And when assets decrease in value, the yield on our new investments should be quite strong.

**Ending Balance**

The third and final benchmark is essential to reaching our ultimate goal, being that the amount of dividend income we can maintain in retirement is a factor of how much wealth we accumulate. Here we're focused on the total value of the portfolio. Is the balance of the portfolio what we should expect it to be at each stage in our investment horizon? If we've met the first two benchmarks, and capital gains keep pace with historic returns, then by default we'll meet the third and final benchmark.

All we have to do is follow the strategy and allow markets to work through their cycles.

**Why aren't capital gains a benchmark?**

You might be asking, if we're going to benchmark our dividends, why aren't we benchmarking our capital gains. When you think about it, there are three components that feed into the ending balance: (1) the amount contributed, (2) our capital gains, and (3) our dividend income.

So why benchmark only two of the three components? We're not necessarily excluding capital gains from our benchmark, but rather we're accounting for it through both investment style and our third benchmark, ending balance.

By investing in index funds, we automatically achieve market returns. So there's nothing to gain by benchmarking these returns. If markets don't perform as expected, we'll see the impact in our ending balance. But there's nothing we can do to compensate for this. If a stock picker misses his benchmark, then he might want to adjust his method of picking stocks. But if markets simply don't perform well, there's no corresponding adjustment for the index fund investor to make (other than to follow through with the rebalancing strategy and let markets recover in due course). There's little that the index fund investor can do if markets don't perform as desired. A new, lower historic average might be set. This is a real possibility. We hope to mitigate the possibility by implementing a long-term investment strategy. But the possibility is real nonetheless.

If trends dictate that markets set new, lower historic averages, then our next best option is to focus on a different benchmark. We can compensate for this by contributing more. We'll discuss this further as we progress through the chapter.

**Let's look at an example**

In *Chapter 5: Asset Allocation* we determined what markets to invest in, the proportion of the portfolio that might be invested in each market, and how those proportions will change as we continually progress towards retirement. Now it's time to take those decisions and plot them out on an amortization table. This will help us visualize where we expect our investments to take us, which in turn provides figures that we can compare our actual results against. As we continue with our long-term investment strategy, we'll want to repeatedly compare our results to the expectations that are plotted on the table. In the example we use annual results for simplicity, though building an amortization table on a quarterly or even monthly basis can provide additional benefits, especially if you intend to rebalance more frequently than once a year.

It should be noted that based on your tolerance for risk and asset allocation, your projected rates of return and dividend yields can be substantially different than what is presented here. It always pays to be conservative. Remember, a market average is just that—*an average.* And your actual results have approximately a 50% chance of coming in below average. In practice I use a rate of 6.125%. This is a conservative approach. It assumes that I'll come in slightly higher than one standard deviation below the average. If over time my portfolio conforms to the historic average, I'll do better than anticipated. But if it comes in more than one standard deviation below the average, then I'll need to make changes to compensate for this, or settle for a smaller retirement than initially projected.

We're going to take a different approach in the following example. Our investor has built a portfolio that rests further to the right on the efficient frontier. But she is still conservative with her benchmarking, meaning that she's prepared to come in a bit below the average. And with time she's going to decrease her tolerance for risk (by increasing the percent of the portfolio allocated to bonds) and further increase her dividend yield (by switching from growth stocks to blue chip stocks and REITs).

It should also be noted that the projected rates of return and dividend yields are realistic long-term averages for this type of investor, but in the short-term results can vary significantly. There will be years when the stock market provides negative returns, and other years when the returns extend into the double digits. The projected rates of return used here assume a smoothing of this affect because we cannot determine when the next crash will occur or for how long any given bull might rage. What we do know is that stocks tend to revert to their mean, which suggests that if the price fluctuates too far from the perceived value in either an up or down direction, a correction will eventually move it back to its perceived value based on a moving average.

We need a benchmark to gauge our results against, but we also know that market conditions can cause our actual results to stray in either direction at any given time before returning to a value that's closer to our expectations. Therefore, the longer we invest, the more likely we are to achieve actual results that conform to a historic long-term average.

You'll see below that the investor intends to contribute $6,000 per year to her portfolio (an equivalent of $500 per month). In the early years she anticipates average capital gains of 7.00% and a dividend yield of 1.50%, for a total annual return of 8.50%.

| Year | Beginning Balance | Contribution | Projected Rate of Return | Capital Gains | Projected Dividend Yield | Dividends | Ending Balance |
|---|---|---|---|---|---|---|---|
| | = ending balance form prior year | amount required to meet long-run investment goal | based on asset allocation and historical returns | = (beginning balance + contribution) x ROR | based on asset allocation and historical long- | = (beginning balance + contributions) x dividend yield | = beginning balance + capital gains + dividends |
| 2020 | - | 6,000.00 | 7.00% | 420.00 | 1.50% | 90.00 | 6,510.00 |
| 2021 | 6,510.00 | 6,000.00 | 7.00% | 875.70 | 1.50% | 187.65 | 13,573.35 |
| 2022 | 13,573.35 | 6,000.00 | 7.00% | 1,370.13 | 1.50% | 293.60 | 21,237.08 |
| 2023 | 21,237.08 | 6,000.00 | 7.00% | 1,906.60 | 1.50% | 408.56 | 29,552.24 |
| 2024 | 29,552.24 | 6,000.00 | 7.00% | 2,488.66 | 1.50% | 533.28 | 38,574.18 |
| 2025 | 38,574.18 | 6,000.00 | 6.50% | 2,897.32 | 1.25% | 557.18 | 48,028.68 |
| 2026 | 48,028.68 | 6,000.00 | 6.50% | 3,511.86 | 1.25% | 675.36 | 58,215.90 |
| 2027 | 58,215.90 | 6,000.00 | 6.50% | 4,174.03 | 1.25% | 802.70 | 69,192.63 |
| 2028 | 69,192.63 | 6,000.00 | 6.50% | 4,887.52 | 1.25% | 939.91 | 81,020.06 |
| 2029 | 81,020.06 | 6,000.00 | 6.50% | 5,656.30 | 1.25% | 1,087.75 | 93,764.11 |
| 2030 | 93,764.11 | 6,000.00 | 6.00% | 5,985.85 | 1.75% | 1,745.87 | 107,495.83 |
| 2031 | 107,495.83 | 6,000.00 | 6.00% | 6,809.75 | 1.75% | 1,986.18 | 122,291.76 |
| 2032 | 122,291.76 | 6,000.00 | 6.00% | 7,697.51 | 1.75% | 2,245.11 | 138,234.37 |
| 2033 | 138,234.37 | 6,000.00 | 6.00% | 8,654.06 | 1.75% | 2,524.10 | 155,412.53 |
| 2034 | 155,412.53 | 6,000.00 | 6.00% | 9,684.75 | 1.75% | 2,824.72 | 173,922.01 |
| 2035 | 173,922.01 | 6,000.00 | 5.50% | 9,895.71 | 2.00% | 3,598.44 | 193,416.16 |
| 2036 | 193,416.16 | 6,000.00 | 5.50% | 10,967.89 | 2.00% | 3,988.32 | 214,372.37 |
| 2037 | 214,372.37 | 6,000.00 | 5.50% | 12,120.48 | 2.00% | 4,407.45 | 236,900.30 |
| 2038 | 236,900.30 | 6,000.00 | 5.50% | 13,359.52 | 2.00% | 4,858.01 | 261,117.82 |
| 2039 | 261,117.82 | 6,000.00 | 5.50% | 14,691.48 | 2.00% | 5,342.36 | 287,151.65 |
| 2040 | 287,151.65 | 6,000.00 | 5.00% | 14,657.58 | 2.25% | 6,595.91 | 314,405.15 |
| 2041 | 314,405.15 | 6,000.00 | 5.00% | 16,020.26 | 2.25% | 7,209.12 | 343,634.52 |
| 2042 | 343,634.52 | 6,000.00 | 5.00% | 17,481.73 | 2.25% | 7,866.78 | 374,983.03 |
| 2043 | 374,983.03 | 6,000.00 | 5.00% | 19,049.15 | 2.25% | 8,572.12 | 408,604.30 |
| 2044 | 408,604.30 | 6,000.00 | 5.00% | 20,730.21 | 2.25% | 9,328.60 | 444,663.11 |
| 2045 | 444,663.11 | 6,000.00 | 4.50% | 20,279.84 | 2.50% | 11,266.58 | 482,209.52 |
| 2046 | 482,209.52 | 6,000.00 | 4.50% | 21,969.43 | 2.50% | 12,205.24 | 522,384.19 |
| 2047 | 522,384.19 | 6,000.00 | 4.50% | 23,777.29 | 2.50% | 13,209.60 | 565,371.08 |
| 2048 | 565,371.08 | 6,000.00 | 4.50% | 25,711.70 | 2.50% | 14,284.28 | 611,367.06 |
| 2049 | 611,367.06 | 6,000.00 | 4.50% | 27,781.52 | 2.50% | 15,434.18 | 660,582.75 |
| 2050 | 660,582.75 | 6,000.00 | 4.00% | 26,663.31 | 2.75% | 18,331.03 | 711,577.09 |
| 2051 | 711,577.09 | 6,000.00 | 4.00% | 28,703.08 | 2.75% | 19,733.37 | 766,013.54 |
| 2052 | 766,013.54 | 6,000.00 | 4.00% | 30,880.54 | 2.75% | 21,230.37 | 824,124.46 |
| 2053 | 824,124.46 | 6,000.00 | 4.00% | 33,204.98 | 2.75% | 22,828.42 | 886,157.86 |
| 2054 | 886,157.86 | 6,000.00 | 4.00% | 35,686.31 | 2.75% | 24,534.34 | 952,378.51 |
| 2055 | 952,378.51 | 6,000.00 | 3.50% | 33,543.25 | 3.00% | 28,751.36 | 1,020,673.12 |
| 2056 | 1,020,673.12 | 6,000.00 | 3.50% | 35,933.56 | 3.00% | 30,800.19 | 1,093,406.87 |
| 2057 | 1,093,406.87 | 6,000.00 | 3.50% | 38,479.24 | 3.00% | 32,982.21 | 1,170,868.32 |
| 2058 | 1,170,868.32 | 6,000.00 | 3.50% | 41,190.39 | 3.00% | 35,306.05 | 1,253,364.76 |
| 2059 | 1,253,364.76 | 6,000.00 | 3.50% | 44,077.77 | 3.00% | 37,780.94 | 1,341,223.47 |

*** The three most important benchmarks for our investor to beat each year, contribution, dividend income, and ending balance, are denoted with beige highlighting.

You'll note that that the investor doesn't use a static rate of return to smooth the results that she expects to receive over her lifetime. Instead, she adjusts her anticipated capital gains and dividend yield as she gradually changes her portfolio allocation. You'll also note that as she decreases her expected capital gains return, she increases her expected dividend yield, yet the dividend yield increases by less than the reduction in expected capital gains. In other words, she's sacrificing growth for safety. The closer she gets to retirement, the more detrimental a crash will be. And for this reason she abandons growth for the safety of bonds, the guaranteed distribution from REITs, and the perceived stability of blue chip stocks.

Her approach becomes more conservative with time, and her expected returns make sense. Come retirement, bonds could make up half the portfolio, and the going yield is contingent on where the Federal Open Market Committee sets interest rates. Bonds might be offering a historically competitive rate, or they might not. We don't know and neither does our investor. But still, she's made a projection, and if need be she can increase her yield by favoring bonds that pay a premium, such as corporate bonds or long-term Treasuries.

It should also be noted that our investor doesn't anticipate a 4% dividend yield. This too should be seen as conservative. Over a 30-year retirement, we expect there to be stretches where a we'll diversified portfolio can easily yield 4%, and times where the investor must choose between reallocating into higher yielding investments or earning less. If she chooses the former, it could force her to eat into principal. This isn't ideal, but still not the end of the world given that the 4% rule assumes that the portfolio will be depleted over time.

In this situation, our investor finishes 2059 with a portfolio valued at $1,341,223. *Not bad!* If she maintains a 3.00% dividend yield she will have annual income of $40,236. By 2059 this likely won't be enough to retire on, but should still serve as a nice complement to Social Security and any other retirement income she's entitled to.

Remember, this is only a projection. And if our investor wants a more comfortable retirement, then she needs to either increase her monthly contribution or work longer. It's her decision. And it's the reason why we make projections this far in advance, just like we did in *Chapter 1: Is $1 Million Enough?*

Now that she's up and running, it's time for our investor to track her performance. She knows how much to contribute each month, and she's benchmarked her ending balance. As a result, she knows how much wealth she'll need to accumulate by the end of each year.

***So what happens if she comes up short?***

Like anything else in the investment world, it depends. If she comes up short in the middle of a bear market, she might not make any changes at all. She'll be invested in stable markets that have a history of always bouncing back. So she'll continue to dollar cost average, all while her dividends are reinvested at great prices. And it's likely that her rebalancing strategy has forced her to recognize at least some gains on her bonds and gold as she rebalances and resultantly buys equities at a discount. The expected rate of return is a long-run average. She should come out of the bear market with strength, but continue to keep an eye on her benchmark as the market recovers.

If, on the other hand, markets are performing well and she's not meeting her benchmark, then changes need to be made.

Perhaps she's invested too heavily in gold. Maybe she's holding more bonds than a woman her age should hold. Or maybe both interest rates and dividend yields are below their historic averages. Whatever the case, she needs to make changes.

The interesting thing about benchmarking against an amount of wealth that you're striving to accumulate—*instead of benchmarking against an index*—is that there's more than one way to get there. Yes, our investor wants to achieve the rate of return that she projects, but it's quite possible that actual returns will fall short. Remember, it's an average, meaning actual result can be either higher or lower. That's why I recommend being conservative with your projections. But regardless of how conservative you are, you can always contribute more money if your ending balance falls short. And if you're able to contribute more money even when you haven't fallen short, *it's even better!*

If our investor is proactive and throws a little extra at the market every time her monthly expenses come in under budget, she increases the probability that she's not going to miss any of her benchmarks. She'll have contributed more, which increases her dividend income, and resultantly increases her ending balance. If she can get some extra momentum in the early years, returns will compound in her favor for an extended period of time. And if she makes an effort to always contribute extra when markets are below their 15-year moving average, she'll be in good position to cross the finish line with significantly more than she anticipates.

Remember what we learned in the first chapter—*it's easy to compensate for a few poor investments with a strong budgeting and savings regimen, but it's nearly impossible to compensate for a lack of savings with superior returns on the stock market.*

**More on Dividends**

In all honesty, the dividend benchmark is my favorite one to track. It might not be as important as your ending balance, especially if you haven't reached the point where you gradually switch over to higher yielding funds, but it's still important nonetheless. It's exciting to watch this number grow. It's fun to watch it get bigger each quarter knowing that it will eventually grow to something you can live on, even if it first grows to something that you could just barely scrape by on. In other words, it provides a sense of security. And once it grows to something you could scrape by on, it will continue to grow. The larger the stream of passive income, the greater the number of shares that you'll acquire each month. This serves to only further increase your dividend income. In dollar terms, your dividend income should continually grow at an increasing rate. That's the power of compounding.

But there's a second reason why I like this benchmark—*during a bear market, this benchmark can provide a psychological benefit.* It's frustrating to watch your portfolio balance decline, especially if it falls below the benchmark. And while contributing more than required will have a tremendous long-term impact, it's hard to buy your way back into the green with an extra hundred dollars or so each month.

Dividends are different. Yields go up when markets are down. It won't make a difference on your existing investments because we track dividends in dollar terms. The fact that yields increase during a bear market is only important to new investors (or more specifically, to new investments). It's the new money that grabs strong yields on beaten down equities. And if we continue to dollar cost average and reinvest our dividends, then we too are throwing new money at the market. And the strong yields on this new money should be felt immediately.

Our ability to beat the dividend benchmark improves during a bear market. We might have to watch the portfolio balance decline for a year or two, but our dividend income will keep getting farther and farther ahead of the benchmark. From a psychological perspective, that's very reassuring.

At the same time, it's important to remember that nothing in life, *or finance*, is guaranteed. Some companies will cut their dividends during a pullback. And the Federal Open Market Committee might reduce interest rates in an effort to stimulate economic activity. Our goal is to diversify away the impact that these types of events bestow.

*For every company that cuts its dividend, how many will continue to increase their dividend?*

If you're invested in the Dividend Aristocrats, you can expect the majority of constituents to increase their dividends annually (the ones that don't will be removed from the index, and funds will be redistributed amongst companies that are able to stay the course). If you're holding REITs, they're required to distribute 90% of their rental income regardless of market conditions. Of course, there's no guarantee that rents won't go down. It all depends on the nature and severity of the pullback. But the fact that they are required to distribute their income is important. And if you hold long-term bond funds, any reduction to the interest rate won't be felt immediately. Existing bonds will continue to cycle through the fund, and will be replaced gradually by new, lower yielding bonds. The immediate impact is that the long-term bond fund will increase in value. Through rebalancing, you'll sell a portion at a gain, and reinvest the proceeds in equities that now offer strong yields.

Each one of these is only an incremental advantage. But that's the point of diversification. We want a host of incremental advantages working in our favor. And we'll recognize the benefits as we track our benchmarks.

So when the bear wreaks havoc, those who track their dividend income should be the first to recognize the benefits. The portfolio might be going through a slump, but it will start disbursing larger streams of income because of that slump. The act of receiving and reinvesting dividends during a bear market will accelerated the rate at which you recover. Eventually, your portfolio will be worth more than it was before the pullback, and this should happen before markets return to their pre-bear-market highs. That's the power of dividend income. Even when capital returns are negative, dividends are always positive. And watching them compound during a bear market should provide the psychological incentive required to see things through.

***Is 30 years enough? And what if she wants to do it in 20 years instead?***

Our investor wants to maximize her income in retirement. And we know that the bigger the pie the bigger the stream of passive income. If our investor can expand her investment horizon by an additional ten years, the results will be astounding. *But is this even possible?* For many, making allocations to a portfolio for 30 years is ambitious. After college we have to pay back student loans (and possibly some credit card debt), buy a house, start a family, *etc. etc. etc.* The list can just keeping getting bigger, and it often will. Because of this, many Americans don't begin a savings regimen until they reach their mid-thirties. Some start even later than that. If our investor starts at age 35 and continues to contribute savings until age 65, we expect her portfolio to be worth $1,341,223. But if she were to live more modestly in her early years (or perhaps work longer in her later years, or maybe some combination of the two), we see that a 40 year investment horizon provides significantly better results. Instead of finishing with $1,341,223 in capital and annual dividend income of $40,236, we expect her to finish with $2,603,890 in capital and annual dividend income of $78,116. The extra 10 years of savings increases her investment horizon by 33.33%, yet her accumulated capital has increased by 94%. Her annual dividend income is also 94% higher. These are amazing results. And it emphasizes the importance of starting young (or if that can't be done, then it emphasizes the importance of starting *now!*).

| Year | Beginning Balance | Contribution | Projected Rate of Return | Capital Gains | Projected Dividend Yield | Dividends | Ending Balance |
|---|---|---|---|---|---|---|---|
| | = ending balance form prior year | amount required to meet long-run investment goal | based on asset allocation and historical returns | = (beginning balance + contribution) x ROR | based on asset allocation and historical long- | = (beginning balance + contributions) x dividend yield | = beginning balance + capital gains + dividends |
| 2059 | 1,253,364.76 | 6,000.00 | 3.50% | 44,077.77 | 3.00% | 37,780.94 | 1,341,223.47 |
| 2060 | 1,341,223.47 | 6,000.00 | 3.50% | 47,152.82 | 3.00% | 40,416.70 | 1,434,792.99 |
| 2061 | 1,434,792.99 | 6,000.00 | 3.50% | 50,427.75 | 3.00% | 43,223.79 | 1,534,444.54 |
| 2062 | 1,534,444.54 | 6,000.00 | 3.50% | 53,915.56 | 3.00% | 46,213.34 | 1,640,573.43 |
| 2063 | 1,640,573.43 | 6,000.00 | 3.50% | 57,630.07 | 3.00% | 49,397.20 | 1,753,600.70 |
| 2064 | 1,753,600.70 | 6,000.00 | 3.50% | 61,586.02 | 3.00% | 52,788.02 | 1,873,974.75 |
| 2065 | 1,873,974.75 | 6,000.00 | 3.50% | 65,799.12 | 3.00% | 56,399.24 | 2,002,173.11 |
| 2066 | 2,002,173.11 | 6,000.00 | 3.50% | 70,286.06 | 3.00% | 60,245.19 | 2,138,704.36 |
| 2067 | 2,138,704.36 | 6,000.00 | 3.50% | 75,064.65 | 3.00% | 64,341.13 | 2,284,110.14 |
| 2068 | 2,284,110.14 | 6,000.00 | 3.50% | 80,153.86 | 3.00% | 68,703.30 | 2,438,967.30 |
| 2069 | 2,438,967.30 | 6,000.00 | 3.50% | 85,573.86 | 3.00% | 73,349.02 | 2,603,890.18 |

*Why are the results so much stronger?* Because the very first $6,000 contribution has now provided returns over a 40 year period instead of a 30 year period. The second $6,000 contributed has now provided returns over a 39 year period instead of a 29 year period, and so forth.

But what if our investor wants to retire early, say in 20 years instead of the 30 to 40 year periods discussed? *Is it possible?* It all comes down to how much she can invest each month, and how the benchmarks might be impacted under a shorter horizon. In our example, 20 years of investing will only produce $ 287,151. This isn't enough to retire on, especially for such a long retirement. But what if she increases her contributions? By doubling the contribution she doubles the results earned over that shortened period, but still doesn't compensate for all those extra years of compounding. She'll finish the 20 years with $ 574,303. Better, but still not enough for an early retirement. She could maintain the level of risk she accepted in the early years—that is, stay in the upper right-hand corner of the efficient frontier without allocating anything to bonds as time passes—and project that her annual return with both capital gains and dividends combined continues at 8.50% for the full 20 years. Then, she can reduce risk to something more reasonable as soon as she reaches retirement. Or she might hope that actual returns are closer to the 10% historic average, or slightly higher, and then work longer if they're not.

The table is included in the download. It's good to play around with the assumptions and see what's possible under different scenarios. In this example the annual contribution is a static $6,000. But in all likelihood our investor's income will increase with inflation, and the annual contribution will likewise increase without putting a strain on her household budget. Or maybe she's moving up the ranks at work and her income will increase by more than the rate of inflation. There's an added benefit to increasing the annual contribution by more than the rate of inflation, and depending on how well she does, this might help her reach retirement in only 20 years. The best advice I can give is to be conservative with your assumptions. When it comes to salary, plan for something close to the industry average, and then increase your benchmark if a promotion comes your way.

**A brief word on taxes**

It should be noted that the example we've discussed completely ignores tax liabilities. As our investor rebalances her portfolio, gains will be recognized. The dividend income could also be subject to taxation.

Taxes are excluded from the example for the simplicity of illustration. Everyone's tax situation is different. Some investors hold their assets in a tax-deferred account while others do not. And some investors have their investments spread amongst multiple accounts with different tax implications. On top of that, interest, rent, and stock dividends all receive different tax treatment.

We won't be discussing taxes here. There's an entire chapter devoted to them in *Dividend Investing*. If you're interested in learning more, then you should have a read. For purposes of *Preparing For Financial Success*, our focus has been on portfolio construction. It's important to acknowledge that any returns recognized outside of a tax-deferred retirement account are subject to taxation. Our strategy is to put proper asset allocation first, and treat taxes as a secondary consideration.

# Chapter 10

## Further Reading

We've covered a lot, haven't we? From cradle to grave, we've seen what the entire investment cycle consists of. It's starts with a forecast, and then we set our goal. We build a budget that allows us to save towards that goal, and implemented an investment strategy aimed at delivering the results we need. We even discussed the theory behind the strategy.

In fact, your eyes might be a little tired. But that doesn't mean your work is done. It just means that a nap might be in your foreseeable future.

Anything worth doing is worth doing right. It's especially true when it comes to building our nest eggs. We can't stop learning here, especially when we consider that markets keep changing. In the previous chapter I stated that investors have better tools at their disposal than ever before in history. Well that's going to change. At the rate technology is advancing, we can only anticipate that the tools will improve. But it's not the only that that will change. New market conditions are going to emerge. Investor behavior will change. The herd will do things that it's never done before. Correlations are going to change. New ones will form. Old ones will go out of vogue. And our friends are going to come up with some crazy insight regarding the next big investment opportunity.

In other words, we're not done learning because much of what we'll need to know hasn't happened yet. The finance world is not static, but constantly evolving. And for that reason, we need to keep reading. One book isn't enough. For an endeavor of this importance, it just couldn't be.

I can't tell you what books to read tomorrow. Many of them haven't been written yet. But I can recommend books that you should read today. They're the same books that I've read, and they're the books I consider most important when it comes to cultivating the approach discussed in *Preparing For Investment Success*.

I'm glad you've read my book and I hope you've learned a lot. But if you only read what one author has to say on the matter, then you're cutting yourself short. I encourage you to not just read what I write, but to also read what I read. The following is a list of the ten books on investing that have influenced me the most.

Even if you subscribe to a different strategy, or plan to implement an altered version of the strategy discussed within, these books are valuable resources. To invest with confidence, you don't just need to study a single strategy, but instead need to study investing as a whole . . . and then implement a strategy that suits your personality the best.

We're fortunate to be following in the footsteps of successful investors. They've written their books, and this allows us to learn what others have learned without repeating mistakes that they've made. As we move into the future, we can only hope that the tradition continues.

**The Intelligent Investor by Benjamin Graham**

This is the oldest book on the list. Ben Graham published *The Intelligent Investor* in 1949, and though much has changed in the financial world, value investors still cherish the work. Of notable importance is the allegory Graham creates with his manic-depressive character *Mr. Market.* He'll tell you exactly what he thinks your stocks are worth today, tomorrow, and the next day. And you'll notice that his temperament fluctuates accordingly.

While I advocate the safety of index funds over individual stocks, when it comes to stock selection, value investing has a lot of merit. It's not day trading and it's not speculating. It's about finding an undervalued company that makes a sustainable product for which demand is expected to persist indefinitely. If you find an undervalued company that makes plastic forks, buy it. That is the heart and soul of value investing.

In *The Intelligent Investor* Graham takes a mathematical approach to stock selection. It's a very detailed and analytical book, and not everyone will consider this an enjoyable read. But as investors it's important to understand our roots. The approach described in *The Intelligent Investor* is very quantitative. And while the lessons contained in this book are exceptional, we should view the material as the foundation on which a modern investment strategy should be built.

Graham's approach worked. He gained followers, and the very act of his followers buying stocks in the manner he describes has impaired the usefulness of his approach. That's what the impact of herd mentality does to a successful investment strategy. The more investors you have searching for value stocks, the fewer the number of values that can be found. Demand for anything will drive up the price. When it comes to value stocks, this kind of demand will reduce the value. When an approach works, the herd will behave in such a way that the benefit is reduced. That's why I recommend this book as a foundation for modern investors. The playing field has changed, but our history has been preserved. This is a book that deserves to be read in such a context.

**A Random Walk Down Wall Street by Burton G. Malkiel**

I've already praised this book. And as far as this list is concerned, it deserves to be the center of attention. This is the book that drives my investment style. Anyone who relies on index funds is a random walker, even if they don't fully understand what it means. Frankly, I don't know where I'd be without the wisdom of Burton G. Malkiel. Perhaps I'd spend countless hours picking my own stocks as I kick myself for never beating the market.

The premise of *A Random Walk* is that the direction of a stock cannot be predicted. As the name implies, it's all random. Yes, there are notable factors that move the price of a stock, be it up or down. But it's only in hindsight that we know which factors have moved which stocks.

Malkiel spends much of the book dissecting well-accepted investment strategies, and a few very outlandish strategies that are used in practice nonetheless. He does this in a manner that is both academic and accessible. You'll get an education in tulip mania, understand why managing a hedge fund isn't much harder than flipping a coin, and you might even be persuaded to fire your financial advisor in favor of a dart-throwing monkey. It all sounds very entertaining– *and it is*–but the lessons contained in this book are invaluable.

In early editions of the 1973 book Malkiel advocated that there should be some mechanism that allows investors to simply hold the market. In 1976 John C. Bogle did just that when his Vanguard Group launched the first index fund, the *Vanguard First Index Investment Trust*, today known as the *500 Index Fund.* Malkiel was certainly ahead of his time–*perhaps only by three years*–but the approach still holds merit.

**Yes, You Can Time the Market! By Ben Stein and Phil DeMuth**

This book also deserves to be on the list, even if mention has already been made. And that's impressive, given that it's a book on market timing. Its redemption value pertains to the fact that it's not a book about making a quick buck. The strategy outlined is so conservative—*and brilliant!*—that it couldn't possibly destroy your portfolio. In fact, the approach can easily improve your performance if implemented over the long-haul.

I've incorporated just a touch of the approach into my strategy. I advocate dollar cost averaging through thick and then, but when markets are down there's definitely an advantage to throwing a little extra money into the portfolio. It's during bear markets when investors stand to gain the most by forgoing their Starbucks in favor of making larger investments.

Stein and DeMuth combine market timing with dollar cost averaging in a manner that works. They implement different entry points for the dollar cost averaging investor to adhere to based on whether or not the market is above or below its moving average. They apply the concept to 100-years-worth of historic data, and repeatedly tweak the approach in order to isolate the variables that most heavily impact the results. It all sounds very mathematical in nature. And it is. But I love Stein's wit, and it's his wit that makes it such an enjoyable read. He has a way of making even the driest, most monotonous subject matter interesting. Of course, most readers are going to be excited by the prospect of making money. It's the 100 years worth of data that would otherwise make most of us yawn.

And if you need a second helping of Stein's wit, make sure you check out *How To Really Ruin Your Financial Life and Portfolio*. It's downright hilarious. And it's the perfect companion to *Yes, You Can Get a Financial Life!* The order that these books should be read in will be different for each investor.

**All About Asset Allocation by Richard Ferri**

This is another book that really hits home the investment strategy that we've discussed. Where Malkiel teaches us why a passive investment strategy is the way to go, Ferri hones in on how different passive investments should be combined inside a single portfolio.

The *All About* series is excellent shopping ground for all investors. With titles such as *All About Market Indicators, All About Dividend Investing, All About Technical Analysis, All About Candlestick Charting, All About Bonds, etc.*, the *All About* series truly has a book for everyone. They cover just about every popular facet of investing. And while some books serve as better compliments than others, there's a benefit to simply learning more. As passive investors we can benefit directly from a book like *All About Exchange-Traded Funds*. But to truly understand the benefits of a passive approach we need to understand the differing strategies that investors implement. There's a reason why some people subscribe to technical analysis, and there's a reason why some people rely on market indicators over a strategy based on periodic rebalancing. By understanding the various approaches available, we are each better prepared to refine a strategy that works for us.

So we read. We follow the market. And at the end of the day we follow the approach that gives us confidence. Of all the books in the *All About* series, *All About Asset Allocation* hits home the hardest. This book will teach you to build a portfolio that provides the maximum return for your tolerated level of risk. It will explain asset correlation and why it's important (yet unpredictable over time). And it will get you on the right path to periodic rebalancing. This is a recommended read for all passive investors.

**Freakonomics: A Rogue Economist Explores the Hidden Side of Everything by Steven D. Levitt and Stephen J. Dubner**

This book doesn't speak specifically to an investment approach. Technically, it's not even a book about investing. Instead, it's a book about human behavior and the impact that this behavior has on our economy. And in that respect, one might conclude that it can substitute as a book on herd mentality.

Investing is a crowd driven activity. It's a group of investors moving in the same direction that carries the price of an investment. And while the contrarian investors often have the last laugh, it takes a tremendous amount of patience, skill, and emotional intelligence to successfully make money as a contrarian.

It truly is the buying and selling done by large institutional investors that move markets, but the propensity of these investors to buy and sell is the culmination of herd mentality.

The herd determines which funds are bought and which funds are sold. Does the public want actively managed funds or passively managed funds? Will the average American start investing before they turn thirty or will they still be paying off debt? If teenagers aren't buying as many cigarettes today, will the healthcare industry be as profitable twenty years from now?

Freakonomics is about crowd behavior and the reward mechanisms that drive said behavior. It's a recommended read for anyone who invests, regardless of style. It's not going to teach you how to invest, but will help you develop a thought process that lends itself well to investing. It all comes down to understanding the herd.

This book is also incredibly entertaining. So if one book isn't enough, can also read *Super Freakonomics*. Both books are highly recommended.

**The Little Book of Common Sense Investing by John C. Bogle**

I love John C. Bogle. In fact, my investment style would not exist without him. I said the same thing about Burton G. Malkiel, but really, the two go hand-in-hand. In early editions of *A Random Walk Down Wall Street*, Malkiel advocates that there should be some mechanism that allows investors to easily invest in the entire market. At the time there was no such thing as an index fund. The only mutual funds available were actively managed, and they charged a hefty fee for the "service."

John Bogle came to our rescue just a short time later, introducing the *Vanguard First Index Investment Trust* in 1976. Today it's known as the *500 Index Fund.* The concept has certainly taken off, as index funds are now available for multiple markets and sectors.

Bogle has authored a number of books, and his investment style has served as subject matter for other authors. I recommend that you start with *The Little Book of Common Sense Investing*. It's particularly useful when read in conjunction with *A Random Walk Down Wall Street.*

**One Up On Wall Street by Peter Lynch**

This book is a good tool for understanding the exact opposite of my approach. If you are going to build a portfolio around individual stocks, the advice in this book is the best you'll find. I encourage you to focus on the number of hours Peter Lynch worked. Through occupation he had a competitive advantage that most individual investors simply don't have. There are only so many hours in a day, and most of us have occupations that are completely unrelated to investing. So in order to solve that problem, Lynch recommends relying on the competitive advantage you gain from your job. You, as a professional, should have a competitive advantage when it comes to identifying the companies in your sector that make for good investments. Even if you're an index fund investor at heart, if you want to allocated just a small portion of your portfolio to individual stocks, *One Up On Wall Street* is a must read.

**Bull! by Maggie Mahar**

This one is written like a novel. Coming in at 532 pages it's an incredibly easy and entertaining read. Even the novice investor will keep turning pages without getting stuck on difficult concepts. It's written in such a way that it just makes sense. When you're done with this, you'll understand how investing is transformed into a game not just by speculators, but by the major players on Wall Street. You'll have a better understanding of how investment cycles work, and you'll understand the type of "*risks*" that fund managers take with the shareholder's money. Hopefully, it will make you appreciate the investment style advocated in *Preparing*

*For Financial Success* all the more . . . and save you the trouble of making some mistakes.

**What Do I Do with My Money Now? edited by Clint Willis**

This is an excellent book for new and experienced investors alike. It's an anthology that doesn't speak to a specific style of investing. Instead, it includes excerpts from some of the most successful investors of our time, each writing about their specific approach to the market. This is an excellent book to determine if the strategy you're following is the right strategy for you.

The book includes writings from Peter Lynch, Warren Buffett, John Templeton, Michael Price, Andrew Tobias, Gary Belsky, and John Rothschild. It's incredibly informative!

**The Four Pillars of Investing by William J. Bernstein**

If you've read (or plan to read) *A Random Walk Down Wall Street*, then you might want to consider *The Four Pillars of Investing* as the perfect companion. Both books advocate an index fund approach . . . and they both paint a grim picture of the mutual fund industry. But what makes *Four Pillars* a companion rather than a substitute is the use of more timely examples. Having come out 29 years after *A Random Walk, Four Pillars* is able to tie the concepts to companies like Enron and groups like The Beardstown Ladies.

Much of it reads like a book of what not to do. But given how simple (yet effective) indexing is, it's difficult to fill too many pages with anecdotes on what the investor should do. The approach is simple yet effective, and easily explained. But all those other approaches that are more likely to put you in the red . . . those are the things you need to spend time learning to avoid.

As the title suggests, it's broken into four sections: theory, history, psychology, and business. These are pillars that all investors should be familiar with, even if their approach is painstakingly simple (yet effective).

## Conclusion

*And there you have it!* You're now ready to get out there on your own. Keep working hard at your day job. It's the fuel that allows you to make the journey towards financial success. But you won't get there on fuel alone. You need a map. And that means you not only need a goal, but a plan on how you're going to get there.

I can't overemphasize how important it is to not only have a budget, but to stick with your budget. When it comes to building wealth, the most important thing you can do is live below your means. You have to spend less than you make, plain and simple.

I hope you've learned a lot. But if you walk away from this book and only remember one thing, I hope you remember that it's nearly impossible to compensate for a lack of savings with superior returns on the stock market. You're in control of how much you save. But average long-term market returns are what they are, and I have no reason to believe that they'll increase significantly in the near future. So hopefully you have a feel for what you can expect to earn in different markets, and will therefore allocate your portfolio according to your tolerance for risk. Rebalance. Reinvest your dividends. Throw extra money at markets when they're trading below their 15-year moving average. Use an amortization table to track your progress. *And that's it!* You're on your way to retirement.

Yes, the approach is simple. That's the beauty behind it. But just because you have a goal, a game plan, and a simple yet effective investment strategy doesn't mean it's time to be lazy. Things change. Markets change. And the financial world will never be static. So keep reading. And please, don't just read what I write. Do yourself a favor and read the books that I've read. We're fortunate to live in a world where the most successful investors of the present and past have written books and created a pool of knowledge from which we can learn.

And books aren't just a great way to learn, but a great way to exercise your brain. It's an incredibly healthy pastime. I hope you don't stop after these 10 books, but make reading a part of your routine, not just as an investor but as a person. As markets change and economic history is made, new books will be written on the subject of investing. And I look forward to reading and writing as much as my time permits.

*Best of luck with your investments!*

## A Final Note to the Reader

Still have questions? That's fine. Investing can pose challenges. There is no single book that will answer all of your questions. Like anything in life, success with your investments is a process of continual learning followed by proper implementation. Don't just read one book about investing. Do what I do and read as many of them as you can.

We have plenty of resources available at www.theselfmadeinvestor.com. We offer tools to help you benchmark and rebalance your portfolio. We publish book recommendations for further reading. The books we recommend are the same books that I've learned from myself, and we only review books that will provide value to our readers. The blog posts, of course, are free. So there's no reason why a fee-conscious index fund investor wouldn't want to pay us a visit.

And if you still have questions, please feel free to shoot me an email: theselfmadeinvestor@gmail.com

As a self-published author I rely on reviews to sell my work. If you feel that the material presented in *Preparing For Financial Success* will provide value to other readers, please leave a review on Amazon or Goodreads. Your support is greatly appreciated!

Made in the USA
Monee, IL
13 September 2026

62981968R00142